INSTANT POT COOKBOOK #2020

550 Easy-to-Remember Quick-to-Make Instant Pot Recipes for Smart People on Any Budget
BY
Francis Michael

ISBN: 978-1-952504-32-7
COPYRIGHT © 2020 by Francis Michael

All rights reserved. This book is copyright protected and it's for personal use only. Without the prior written permission of the publisher, no part of this publication should be reproduced, distributed, or transmitted in any form or by any means, including photocopying, recording, or other electronic or mechanical methods.

This publication is sold with the idea that the publisher is not required to render accounting, officially permitted, or otherwise, qualified services. Seek for the services of a legal or professional, a practiced individual in the profession if advice is needed.

DISCLAIMER

The information contained in this book is geared for educational and entertainment purposes only. Concerted efforts have been made towards providing accurate, up to date and reliable complete information. The information in this book is true and complete to the best of our knowledge.

Neither the publisher nor the author takes any responsibility for any possible consequences of reading or enjoying the recipes in this book. The author and publisher disclaim any liability in connection with the use of information contained in this book. Under no circumstance will any legal responsibility or blame be apportioned against the author or publisher for any reparation, damages, or monetary loss due to the information herein, either directly or indirectly.

Table of Contents

- INTRODUCTION 8
- What is an Instant Pot? 8
- Benefits of Cooking with an Instant Pot 9
- Function Buttons of Your Instant Pot 11
- Steps to Effectively Clean Your Instant Pot 14
- INSTANT POT BREAKFAST RECIPES 16
  - Breakfast Cobbler 16
  - Cinnamon Banana Oatmeal 17
  - Quinoa Blueberry Breakfast Bowl 18
  - Buckwheat Porridge 19
  - Apple Cinnamon Oatmeal Cup 20
  - Strawberry Trail Mix Oatmeal 21
  - Breakfast Burrito Casserole 22
  - Crustless Tomato Spinach Quiche 23
  - Jamaican Cornmeal Porridge 24
  - Steel Cut Oatmeal 25
  - Lemon Blueberry Breakfast Cake 26
  - Spanish Chorizo Breakfast Hash 27
  - Banana Oatmeal 28
  - Breakfast Quinoa 29
  - Macaroni and Cheese 30
  - Spiced Apple Steel Cut Oats 31
  - Fajita Breakfast Casserole 32
  - Chocolate Bircher Muesli 33
  - Blueberry Oatmeal 34
  - Vanilla Apple Cinnamon Breakfast Quinoa 35
  - Chocolate Steel Cut Oats 36
  - Double Berry Oatmeal 37
- INSTANT POT SOUP & STEW RECIPES 38
  - Italian Wedding Soup 38
  - Mexican Chicken Stew 39
  - Minestrone Soup 40
  - Brunswick Stew 41

- Tomato Basil Soup 42
- Cuban Shredded Beef Stew 43
- Broccoli Cheese Soup 44
- Spicy Ethiopian Stew 45
- Cheeseburger Soup 46
- Andouille Sausage Stew 47
- Potato Leek Soup 48
- Hoppin' John Stew 49
- French Onion Soup 50
- Irish Stew 51
- Chicken Noodle Soup 52
- Cheddar Broccoli & Potato Soup 53
- Italian Beef Stew 54
- Swiss Chard Stem Soup 55
- Apple Spice Beef Stew 56
- Spanish Infused Chicken Stew 57
- Red Pepper Tomato Soup 58

INSTANT POT FISH & SEAFOOD RECIPES 59

- Brazilian Fish Stew 59
- Salmon Croquettes 60
- Fish Coconut Curry 61
- Lemon Dill Salmon 62
- Steamed Alaskan Crab Legs 63
- Manhattan Clam Chowder 64
- Lemon Scented Fish Broth 65
- Salmon Tortellini Soup 66
- Lemon Garlic Parmesan Shrimp Pasta 67
- Tomato Pasta with Tuna & Capers 68
- Lemon Pepper Salmon 69
- Teriyaki Salmon 70
- Tuna Noodle Casserole 71
- Seafood Corn Chowder 72
- Shrimp & Pasta 74
- 10-Minute Instant Pot Salmon 75

New England Clam Chowder 76

INSTANT POT POULTRY RECIPES 77

Hawaiian Shredded Chicken 77

Salsa Lime Chicken 78

Chicken Quinoa Casserole 79

Honey Garlic Chicken 80

Creamy Italian Chicken Breasts 81

Chicken Marsala 82

White Chicken Chili 83

Chicken Cordon Bleu 84

Orange Chicken 85

Pineapple Chicken Breasts 86

BBQ Chicken with Potatoes 87

Spicy Honey Chicken 88

Chicken Parmesan Casserole 89

INSTANT POT BEAN & RICE RECIPES 90

Coconut Rice Pudding 90

Refried Beans 91

American Spanish Rice 92

Cinnamon Brown Rice Pudding 93

Mexican Beef Rice 94

13 Bean Soup 95

Millet & Pinto Bean Chili 96

Rice Pudding 97

Yellow Rice with Peas & Corn 98

Red Beans and Rice 99

Baked Beans 100

Rice Pilaf 101

INSTANT POT LAMB, BEEF & PORK RECIPES 102

Red Wine Beef Stew 102

Asian Pork 103

Italian Beef 104

Smoky Pork and Hominy Soup 105

Beef Sirloin Tips 106

Thai Lettuce Pork Wraps 107

Mexican Shredded Beef 108

Salsa Pork Chops 109

Easy Beef Stew 110

Barbacoa Pulled Pork 111

Beef Curry 112

Tender Greek Pork 113

Beef Stroganoff 114

Teriyaki Pork Loin 115

Beef Short Ribs 116

Pork Loin, Stuffing & Gravy 117

Corned Beef and Cabbage 118

Japanese Pork Tender Rib Stew 119

Beef Masala Curry 120

INSTANT POT EGG RECIPES 121

Bacon and Egg Risotto 121

Hard Boiled Eggs 122

Egg Bake 123

Crustless Quiche 124

Eggs en Cocotte 125

Ham and Egg Casserole 126

Mini Fiittatas 127

Perfect Poached Egg 128

Cheesy Eggs 129

French "Baked" Eggs 130

Mexican Casserole 131

INSTANT POT VEGAN & VEGETARIAN RECIPES 132

Vegetable Beef Soup 132

Lentil Coconut Curry 133

Vegan Quinoa Burrito Bowls 134

Bulgogi Mushroom Lettuce Wraps 135

Cauliflower Tikka Masala 136

Cilantro Lime Quinoa 137

Vegan Alfredo Sauce 138

- Vegetable Bolognese 139
- Mashed Potatoes with Fried Onions and Bacon 140
- Berry Jam 141
- Maple Bourbon Chili 142

INSTANT POT APPETIZER RECIPES 143
- Apple Bread with Salted Caramel Icing 143
- Cheesy Tuna Helper 144
- Cornbread Taco Pie 145
- French Onion Pot Roast 146
- Chicken Pot Pie Casserole 147
- South West burritos 148
- Bacon and Ranch Salad 149
- Cheesy Taco Pasta 150
- Homemade Lasagna Hamburger Helper 151
- Loaded Corn Chowder 152

INSTANT POT DESSERT RECIPES 153
- Chocolate Pudding Cake 153
- Pineapple Upside Down Cake 154
- Key Lime Pie 155
- Samoa Cheesecake made with Ricotta 156
- Pumpkin Banana Chocolate Chip Bundt Cake 157
- Crème Brulee 158
- Chocolate Lava Cake 159
- Lemon Blueberry Breakfast Cake 160
- Cookies & Cream Cheesecake 161

INTRODUCTION

What is an Instant Pot?

The Instant Pot is an electronic cooking device or machine programmed to perform the function of 7 gadgets. Unlike electric pressure cooker, steamer, slow cooker, yoghurt maker, rice cooker, warming pot or sauté pan, Instant Pot is a cooker programmed with multi-functions which can perform the same task like the afore mentioned machines. The Instant Pot is a seven-in-one multi cooker combined that can work as an electric pressure cooker, steamer, slow cooker, yoghurt maker, rice cooker, and sauté pan. It can cook meals instantly and faster but it has an option for a start time that can be programmed to delay.

Some people that likes convenient cooking and the option of "set it and forget it" in a slow cooker would have a great passion for Instant Pot and also including those who desires to have a pressure cooker, steamer, yoghurt maker and slow cooker simultaneously but has little or no space to occupy the four cookers, Instant Pot performs the same functions like the other four machines. The Instant Pot comes with instruction manual and short booklet of recipes which contain functions of Instant Pot and manufacturer's recommended quantities of food ingredients together with preparation and cooking times to help the newbies.

The Instant Pot will save you a whole lot of time if you want to cook food like stew, lentils or grains. The special thing about Instant Pot is that it has a lot of functional uses for a single appliance and you can set it and walk away doing other things while the machine does its magic. With its multi-functional ability, it may seem difficult to operate your Instant Pot but it's very easy to operate when you follow the instruction manual.

Benefits of Cooking with an Instant Pot

1. **It Can Cook Beans Super-Fast.**

This reason alone got my attention to this fabulous Instant Pot device. While it takes some people about 12-15 minutes to cook soaked beans and 37-40 minutes to cook dry beans. I was not fully convinced when the Instant Pot cook beans very fast until I heard it over and over again from different people and their good comments made about their Instant Pot. That was when I started having great passion for Instant Pot and it earned a space in my kitchen.

2. **To Make Perfect Brown Rice.**

It's not easy to cook brown rice but it was easy for me. I have been thinking brown rice was easy to cook but was doubtful the first time I cooked brown rice with little water and I thought I would made crunchy rice. However, the rice was not crunchy as I thought and it was perfect rice I have ever cooked. You can use your Instant Pot to make recipes like Mexican Casserole, Cheesy Broccoli and Rice Casserole perfectly in a fraction of the time.

3. **Steam/Cook Veggies in Minutes.**

The Instant Pot cooks veggies in minutes. When cooking veggies, do not walk away to avoid burning or overcooking your veggies. It's important to stick to the step by step recipes instructions when cooking veggies. I've burned more than my fair share of veggies by forgetting about them. You have to make use of quick pressure release to release the steam once they are finished cooking.

4. **Built in Timer.**

What amazes me the most about the Instant Pot machine is the fact that you can cook a meal, walk away and come back later to meet fully cooked meals. The Instant Pot will not start cooking by itself until you want it to cook by using the timer. You can program your dinner to start at 4:30pm and keep it warm until you get home.

5. **Easy Clean Up.**

Washing of my dishes is one of the things I have little time to do. I do avoid cooking dishes that will require thorough washing of dishes. When it comes to Instant Pot, it is very easy to clean up after use.

6. **Pressure Cooking Retains More Nutrients.**

Researchers have it that food cooked for a short time with less water retains more nutrients. Instant Pot retains more nutrients because of its short duration used for cooking. Due to the high pressure, beans and grains become more digestible.

7. **They are Safe.**

There are some reports on injuries or dangers of pressure cookers blowing up while cooking. Some people became scared of using pressure cooker because of some domestic violence caused by the pressure cooker. However, Instant Pot is very safe to use. It has 10 in-built safety features which include high temperature warning, a lid which is to be locked while cooking, automatic pressure control and many others.

8. **Slow Cooker.**

The Instant Pot is a little taller but has the same size with slow cookers. The Instant Pot also perform the function of a slow cooker by just pressing a button. Some people may decide to use their Instant Pot as a slow cooker on regular bases. By doing this, you must make sure you buy the optional lid so you can be able to use the Instant Pot as a slow cooker on regular basis.

9. **Sauté feature.**
The Instant Pot has a sauté feature. It means the Instant Pot can also perform the function of a sauté pan. So you can toss onions and garlic in, select sauté button, prepare the rest of your ingredients and then add them to the pot and set the time you want Instant Pot to cook whatever you wants to cook.

Function Buttons of Your Instant Pot

1. **Manual / Pressure Buttons:**
   This function will be frequently used which enables you to select the cooking time manually and pressure cook what you wants to cook. The Instant Pot pressure, time and temperature can be adjusted by pressing the "+/-" features. It is imperative to follow the recipe instructions to know if you are to pressure cook the food using Low or High Pressure. The "Manual" and "Pressure" button stands for pressure cooking unlike functions like "Sauté", "Yogurt" or "Slow cooker" which does not require pressure cooking. The Instant Pot's default setting is High Pressure when you press the "Manual" button.

2. **Sauté Button:**
   This feature is the second most frequently used button on the Instant Pot. You can select the sauté button to cook up anything as you would in a skillet or pan without 1 cup of liquid. All you need to do is just to set the "Sauté" button, add some cooking oil like butter, avocado, coconut or animal fat like beef tallow or lard to the inner pot and add food you want to cook like a skillet or pan. The sauté button can be used to cook ingredients like onion, garlic and meat. Most times, I start with the "Sauté" function and then use the "Manual" / "Pressure" button to pressure cook my meal.

3. **Slow Cook Button:**
   This button helps you to use Instant Pot like a slower cooker. This function allows the Instant Pot to perform the function of a slow cooker. Just add food as you normally do to a slow cooker, secure the lid and then select the "Slow Cook" button and use "+/-" buttons to adjust the cook time.

4. **Bean / Chili:**
   This button allows the Instant Pot to cook beans faster than any other cooker. This is why beans is the food I like cooking most in my Instant Pot. The "Bean / Chili" button, uses the default High Pressure for 30 minutes though it can be adjusted for "More" to High Pressure for 35 minutes or "Less" for High Pressure for 20 minutes. Black beans take about 10-15 minutes, while kidney beans take 20-25. The Instant Pot Manual has different cooking times for various beans and legumes.

5. **Meat / Stew:**
   The Instant Pot can easily make your favorite stew or meat dish. It can make it by adjusting the settings depending on the desired texture. For instance, a homemade stew with about 1-2 lb. of meat, you can set it to "Meat / Stew" button using high pressure for 35 minutes. The "More" setting is great for fall-off-the-bone cooking. It will set to a default High Pressure for 35 minutes. The Instant Pot can be adjusted for "More" to High Pressure for 45 minutes or "Less" for High Pressure for 20 minutes.

6. **Multigrain:**
   This function can be used for cooking wild rice or brown rice which usually takes longer time than cooking white rice. Cook brown rice to a 1:1.25 ratio rice to water and wild rice to a 1:3 ratio rice to water for 25-30 minutes. The default (Normal) setting is 40 minutes of cooking time but can be adjusted as required for the "Less" setting to 20 minutes of cooking time, or "More" at 45 minutes of warm water soaking and 60 minutes of cooking.

7. **Porridge:**

Rice porridge (congee) and other grains can be cooked using the porridge button. The default cooking time on High Pressure for rice porridge is 20 minutes but can be adjusted for "More" to High Pressure for 30 minutes or "Less" for High Pressure for 15 minutes. When the cooking cycle has completed, it is not advisable to use Quick Pressure Release because it has high starch content and may splatter the porridge through the steam release vent. It's imperative to use the Natural Pressure Release to release the steam.

8. **Poultry:**

This button can be used for making chicken and other poultry recipes in the Instant Pot. The default cooking program is 15 minutes but can be adjusted for "More" to High Pressure for 30 minutes or "Less" for High Pressure for 5 minutes. I always make shredded chicken for homemade tacos and burrito bowls. Add about 1 lb. uncooked chicken, ¼ cup of homemade salsa, 1 cup of bone broth, 1 tsp. cumin, 1 clove garlic minced, ½ tsp oregano, ½ onion, and $1/8$ tsp. paprika into the bottom of your Instant Pot. Secure the lid in place and select the "Poultry" button to the default at High Pressure for 15 minutes. When the cooking cycle has finished, do a Natural Pressure Release for 10 minutes. Carefully open the lid, shred the chicken the two forks, add pepper and salt to taste.

9. **Rice:**

This button is used to cook rice in your Instant Pot using half the time a conventional rice cooker could use. It uses about 4 to 8 minutes, short grain, Jasmine, White rice, and Basmati rice can all be cooked using this function. You'll need a 1:1 ratio of rice to water (Basmati is a 1:1.5 ratio). It depends on the quantity of food you want to cook on low pressure, when you press the "Rice" button, the cooking duration automatically adjusts. It's always necessary to add further 10-12 minutes to the cooking time to allow the Instant Pot to come to pressure but cooking rice in the "Manual" mode at high pressure is my frequent selection. I usually add 1:1 ratio of rice to water into the bottom of my Instant Pot and set to 3 minutes with a 12 minute Natural Pressure Release when the timer beeps..

10. **Soup:**

Soup, stock, and broth can be made using the "Soup" button. Water doesn't heavily boil because Instant Pot will control the pressure and temperature so that the liquid doesn't heavily boil. You can adjust the cooking time as required, usually between 20-40 minutes, and the pressure to either Low or High Pressure. Anytime you wish to make homemade bone broth faster than the conventional slow cooker, it is very simple. Click the "Soup" button, set the Low Pressure, and set the cooking time to 120 minutes. Once the timer beeps, do Natural Pressure Release to release the steam.

11. **Steam:**

This button can be used to steam vegetables, seafood or reheat food. Always use the steam rack of your Instant Pot when steaming veggies to avoid burning and sticking to the bottom of your Instant Pot. Add 1-2 cups of water to the inner liner, place the steam rack inside the inner pot and with a stainless steel steam basket on top. Add the vegetables, seafood, etc. in the basket. Select the "Steam" button and then adjust the time using the "+" or "-" key. When you are cooking foods like frozen corn on the cob or a fresh fish filet, adjust the time to 3-5 minutes and 8-10 minutes if you are cooking fresh artichokes could take 9-11 minutes.

12. **Keep Warm Button:**

This button is used to keep food hot when the Instant Pot is done with cooking or to cancel the pressure cooking mode. Immediately cooking time is finished, the Instant Pot will beep and automatically go into the "Keep Warm" function. It will display an "L" in front of a number to indicate how long it's been warm – e.g. "L0:30" for 30 minutes. This button helps to keep food warm (145 to 172°F) for up to 99 hours, 50 minutes.

13. **Cancel Button:**

If by mistake you selected wrong cooking time and you want to stop cooking or adjust pressure cooking time, you can cancel and return to standby mode by selecting the "Keep Warm" / "Cancel" button.

14. **Timer Button**

This button can be used to delay the cooking start time for the Instant Pot for both pressure cooking and slow cook options. Press the Timer button with 10 seconds of pressing Pressure / Manual button or Slow Cook button. To adjust the delayed hours, Use "+/-" buttons then wait a second and press Timer again to set delayed minutes. Press the Keep Warm / Cancel button to cancel the Timer anytime.

Steps to Effectively Clean Your Instant Pot

Step 1: Unplug:

Before you start cleaning your Instant Pot, make sure it is unplugged. It's advisable to unplug your Instant Pot whenever it's not in use. For this purpose, you have to make sure it's unplugged for the intensive cleaning you're about to do, for the safety of your Instant Pot and for your safety too.

Step 2: Cleaning housing unit:

The outside housing unit cannot go into the dishwasher so you should be able to clean it thoroughly with a rag. Get the rag good and damp with water and cleaning solution, and wipe down both the interior and exterior parts of the main housing unit. To have a perfect cleaning, a sponge is recommended to get those hard or stiff food bits and mineral deposits. Don't fail to clean everywhere you may have tiny particles.

Step 3: Wash the lid:

The lid has to be washed properly. This can be done by washing it in the sink with warm water with a little dish soap to make all the residuals are removed because this can contaminate. Some people used a vinegar solution to remove the unpleasant smell from residuals.

Step 4: Check other crevices:

There are some parts in the Instant Pot that you might not like to cleaning all the time you are washing the Instant Pot. Get all those crevices and small parts where food residue may build up for some period of time. Remove the Quick Release handle, and wash it with warm-soapy water. In some cases, the steam valve can get blocked if too much deposit builds up there. Remove the shield, located inside the lid which blocks the valve. The shield could pop off easily depending on the model your Instant Pot. Wash the shield in the sink. Check the condensation collection cup at the side of your Instant Pot. It might have collected food residue over time. If it has some residue on it, clean it in the sink.

Step 5: clean sealing ring:

The silicone ring found on the underside of the lid will likely need a thorough cleaning. This is what indicates your Instant Pot has a tight seal, and it's an easy spot for food particles or residual smells to lurk. Check it for any signs of damage, as silicone can start to crack over time. If you notice any crack in the silicone ring, it has been damaged and needs a replacement immediately. The silicone ring is dishwasher-safe, so you can pop it in there on the top rack. Once it's thoroughly cleaned, place it back on the underside of the lid, and make sure you've got a secure fit.

Step 6: Wash the inner pot:

The inner pot is dishwasher-safe. With this fact, you should be washing the inner pot at regularly intervals. Since you're doing a deep clean, it doesn't hurt to pop the inner pot into the dishwasher together with any of the other dishwasher-safe parts you use with your Instant Pot, such as silicone molds and wire racks. When you finished washing the inner pot, dry it off using a paper towel or use some household vinegar to give it a thorough wipe-down. By doing this, it can get rid of any accumulated residue from things like minerals in your water, or dish detergent. This will make your Instant Pot looks shiny and nice.

Step 7: Steam clean and let dry:

At this stage, you have done a thorough cleaning, reassemble all the parts. Don't forget about those small parts like the sealing ring and shield because they can be missed easily. The purpose of this washing and cleaning is to ensure your Instant Pot is safe so you can use it for a long period of time. However, after doing all the washing and cleaning but you realized the sealing ring still has a strange food smell, you may need to deodorize the part with a vinegar steam clean. The process is simple and can be done directly in the Instant Pot by adding a cup of water, a cup of vinegar, and some lemon peels (for extra freshness!) to the inner pot, press "Steam" button and set for a few minutes. When the timer beeps, do a natural pressure release. Open the lid, remove the sealing ring and dry it at a convenient place.

INSTANT POT BREAKFAST RECIPES

Breakfast Cobbler

Serves: 2
Preparation time: 10 minutes
Cook time: 10 minutes
Total time: 20 minutes

Ingredients:
- 1 pear, diced
- 1 apple, diced
- 1 plum, diced
- 2 tablespoons (30 ml) local honey
- 3 tablespoons (45 ml) coconut oil
- ½ teaspoon of ground cinnamon
- ¼ cup (19 g) unsweetened shredded coconut
- ¼ cup (30 g) pecan pieces
- 2 tablespoons (20 g) sunflower seeds (salted and roasted will work)
- Coconut whipped cream, for garnish

Cooking Instructions:
1. Add the cut fruit into the bottom of your Instant Pot.
2. Add in the honey and coconut oil, and sprinkle the cinnamon.
3. Close and lock the lid in place. Select the Steam function to cook for 10 minutes. When the timer beeps, do a quick pressure release.
4. Carefully open the lid and transfer the cooked fruit with a slotted spoon into medium bowl.
5. Add coconut, pecans, and sunflower seeds into the residual liquid in the pot. Select the Sauté function and leave the contents to cook, turning them regularly to avoid burning.
6. Remove them and top with the fruit when they are nicely browned and toasted for about 5 minutes.
7. Serve warm and topped with coconut whipped cream if desired.

Cinnamon Banana Oatmeal

Preparation time: 20 minutes
Cook time: 5 minutes
Total time: 25 minutes
Servings: 3

Ingredients:
- 1 cup of old fashioned oatmeal
- 1 cup of milk
- 1 cup of water
- 2 bananas
- 2 teaspoons of cinnamon
- 1 tablespoon of brown sugar

Cooking Instructions:
1. Use a non-stick cooking spray to spray the bottom of your Instant Pot.
2. Place in the oatmeal, milk and water. Slice 1 of the bananas and place it into the bottom of your Instant Pot.
3. Add in cinnamon and brown sugar and give everything a good stir. Close and lock the lid in place. Select Manual, High Pressure for 5 minutes.
4. When the timer beeps, do a natural pressure release for about 10 minutes, then quick release any remaining pressure.
5. Carefully open the lid and stir the oatmeal. Scoop into individual serving bowls. Slice the second banana and add fresh slices to the top of each bowl.
6. Serve and enjoy!

Quinoa Blueberry Breakfast Bowl

Preparation time: 5 minutes
Cook time: 1 minute
Total time: 5 minutes
Servings: 4
Calories: 400 kcal

Ingredients:
- 1 ½ cups of white quinoa, rinsed in a fine mesh strainer
- 1 ½ cups of water
- 1 cinnamon stick
- ¼ cup of raisins
- 1 tbsp. of honey, plus more for serving
- ¾ cup of grated apple
- 1 cup of cold-pressed apple juice
- 1 cup of plain yogurt plus more for serving
- ¼ cup of chopped pistachios
- Blueberries to serve

Cooking Instructions:
1. Place the rinsed quinoa, water and cinnamon stick into the bottom of your Instant Pot. Close and lock the lid in place. Select Manual, High Pressure for 1 minute.
2. When the timer beeps, do a natural pressure release, then quick release any remaining pressure. Carefully open the lid.
3. Transfer the quinoa into a medium bowl. Lift out the cinnamon stick and let to cool. Add the raisins, honey, apple and apple juice.
4. Give everything a good stir to combine. Refrigerate for at least 1 hour or overnight. Add the yogurt and give everything a good stir to combine.
5. Serve topped with yogurt, pistachios, blueberries and honey.

Buckwheat Porridge

Preparation time: 5 minutes
Cook time: 25 minutes
Total time: 30 minutes
Servings: 4

Ingredients:
- 1 cup of raw buckwheat groats, rinsed
- 3 cups of rice milk
- 1 banana, sliced
- ¼ cup of raisins
- 1 teaspoon of ground cinnamon
- ½ teaspoon of vanilla
- Chopped nuts, optional

Cooking Instructions:
1. Add the rinsed buckwheat groats into the bottom of your Instant Pot.
2. Add the rice milk, banana, raisins, cinnamon and vanilla. Close and lock the lid in place and ensure that the valve is in sealing position.
3. Select Manual, High Pressure for 6 minutes. When the timer beeps, do a natural pressure release for about 20 minutes.
4. Carefully remove the lid and give the porridge a good stir with a long-handled spoon.
5. Add more rice milk to individual servings until your desired consistency is achieved. Sprinkle with chopped nuts if desired.
6. Serve and enjoy!

Apple Cinnamon Oatmeal Cup

Preparation time: 10 minutes
Cook time: 10 minutes
Total time: 20 minutes

Ingredients:
- ½ cup of oatmeal
- 1/3 cup of coconut or almond milk
- ¼ teaspoon of baking powder
- ¼ teaspoon of cinnamon
- ½ teaspoon of vanilla
- 1 teaspoon of maple syrup (optional)
- 1 egg
- ¼ cup of diced apples

Cooking Instructions:
1. Add all of the ingredients in a coffee mug. Give everything a good mix until all of the oatmeal is wet.
2. Pour 2 cups of water into the bottom of your Instant Pot and place the trivet. Add the coffee mug in the Instant Pot.
3. Close and lock the lid in place and ensure that the valve is in sealing position. Select Manual, High Pressure for 10 minutes.
4. When the timer beeps, do a natural pressure release for about 10 minutes. Carefully open the lid and remove the mug.
5. Serve warm and enjoy!

Strawberry Trail Mix Oatmeal

Preparation time: 5 minutes
Cook time: 10 minutes
Total time: 15 minutes
Servings: 2

Ingredients:

- 1 cup of steel cut oats
- 1.5 cups of water
- 2 tablespoons of butter
- 1 cup of freshly squeezed orange juice
- 1 tablespoon of dried cranberries
- 1 tablespoon of raisins
- 1 tablespoon of chopped dried apricots
- 2 tablespoons of pure maple syrup
- ¼ teaspoon of ground cinnamon
- 2 tablespoons of chopped pecans
- 1/8 teaspoon of salt
- **Tasty Toppings:** ½ - 1 cup chopped strawberries, Extra cinnamon, Extra pecans, Any additional fruit or sweetener, Milk or almond milk, Granola

Cooking Instructions:

1. Spray the inner liner of your Instant Pot with non-stick cooking spray.
2. Add all of the ingredients into the bottom of your Instant Pot except for toppings and give everything a good stir to combine.
3. Close and lock the lid in place and ensure that the valve is in sealing position. Select Manual, High Pressure for 10 minutes.
4. When the timer beeps, do a quick pressure release. Carefully open the lid and stir the oatmeal.
5. Spoon the cooked oats into two bowls and add on your favorite toppings.
6. Serve and enjoy!

Breakfast Burrito Casserole

Preparation time: 10 minutes
Cook time: 13 minutes
Total time: 23 minutes
Serving: 6 tacos

Ingredients:
- 4 eggs
- 2 lb. red potatoes, cubed
- ¼ cup of chopped white or yellow onion
- 1 diced jalapeno
- 6 ounce of ham steak, cubed
- ½ teaspoon of salt
- ½ teaspoon of mesquite seasoning
- ¼ teaspoon of chili powder
- ¾ teaspoon of taco seasoning
- Burrito toppings: Salsa, avocado, hot sauce and marinated red onions.
- Tortillas: new Siete coconut flour

Cooking Instructions:
1. Mix together the salt, seasonings and eggs and 1 tbsp. of water in a medium bowl. Lightly beat the eggs until the yokes are broken up.
2. Place the onions, potatoes or cheese, ham and jalapeno into the bowl. Add the mixture in a metal bowl. Cover the metal bowl with a piece of aluminum foil.
3. Pour 1 cup of water into the bottom of your Instant Pot and place the trivet. Add the metal bowl containing egg mixture into the trivet.
4. Close and lock the lid in place. Select Manual, High Pressure for 13 minutes. When the timer beeps, do a natural pressure release for about 15 minutes.
5. Carefully open the lid and remove the pan from your Instant Pot. Fill your burritos! In a skillet, heat up the tortillas for a couple of seconds on each side.
6. In each burrito, add a few scoops of the egg mixtures, a slice of avocado, salsa and red onions. Wrap up and enjoy.
7. Serve and enjoy!

Crustless Tomato Spinach Quiche

Preparation time: 10 minutes
Cook time: 20 minutes
Total time: 30 minutes

Ingredients:
- 12 large eggs
- ½ cup of milk
- ½ tsp. of salt
- ¼ tsp. of fresh ground black pepper
- 3 cups of fresh baby spinach, roughly chopped
- 1 cup of diced seeded tomato
- 3 large green onions, sliced
- 4 tomato slices, for topping
- ¼ cup of shredded Parmesan cheese

Cooking Instructions:
1. Place a trivet into the bottom of your Instant Pot and pour 1 ½ cups of water.
2. In a medium bowl, whisk together the eggs, milk, salt and pepper. Add the spinach, tomato, and green onions to a 1 ½ quart baking dish and give everything a good mix.
3. Pour the egg mixture over the veggies and give everything a good stir to combine. Carefully add sliced tomatoes on top and sprinkle with Parmesan cheese.
4. Place the dish on the trivet with a sling. Close and lock the lid in place and ensure that the valve is in sealing position.
5. Select Manual, High Pressure for 20 minutes. When the timer beeps, do a natural pressure release for about 10 minutes, then quick release any remaining pressure.
6. Carefully remove the lid and take out the dish from your Instant Pot. Add in a broiler and broil until lightly browned if desired.
7. Serve and enjoy!

Jamaican Cornmeal Porridge

Preparation time: 5 minutes
Cook time: 20 minutes
Total time: 25 minutes
Yield: 4

Ingredients:
- 4 cups of water, separated
- 1 cup of milk
- 1 cup of yellow cornmeal, fine
- 2 sticks of cinnamon
- 3 pimento berries
- 1 teaspoon of vanilla extract
- ½ teaspoon of nutmeg, ground
- ½ cup of sweetened condensed milk

Cooking Instructions:
1. Pour 3 cups of water and 1 cup of milk into the bottom of your Instant pot.
2. In a separate bowl, whisk together 1 cup of water and cornmeal until they are combined. Pour the mixture into your Instant Pot and whisk.
3. Add the cinnamon sticks, pimento berries, vanilla extract, and nutmeg. Close and lock the lid in place and ensure that the valve is in sealing position.
4. Select the Porridge button to cook for 6 minutes. When the timer beeps, do a natural pressure release for about 10 minutes.
5. Carefully open the lid and add the sweetened condensed milk to sweeten.
6. Serve immediately and enjoy!

Steel Cut Oatmeal

Preparation time: 5 minutes
Cook Time: 10 minutes
Total time: 15 minutes
Serving: 1

Ingredients:
- 1/3 cup of steel cut oats
- 1/3 cup of milk
- ½ cup of water
- 1 ½ teaspoon of brown sugar

Cooking Instructions:
1. Use a non-stick cooking spray to spray the bottom of your Instant Pot.
2. Add in the oats, milk, water and brown sugar and give everything a good stir.
3. Close and lock the lid in place and ensure that the valve is in sealing position. Select Manual, High Pressure for 10 minutes.
4. When the timer beeps, do a quick pressure release. Carefully open the lid and spoon your oatmeal into a bowl.
5. You can also serve with sliced bananas and a splash of milk.
6. Serve and enjoy!

Lemon Blueberry Breakfast Cake

Preparation time: 20 minutes
Cook time: 30 minutes
Total time: 60 minutes
Servings: 2 small cakes

Ingredients:
- 2 cups of unbleached all-purpose flour
- 2 tsp. of baking powder
- ½ tsp. of salt
- 1 lemon, zest
- ½ cup of unsalted butter, room temp
- ¾ cup of sugar
- 1 egg, room temp
- 1 tsp. of vanilla extract
- ½ cup of buttermilk (or any milk with 1 tbsp. of lemon juice)
- 2 cups of fresh or frozen blueberries
- ½ lemon, juice, optional
- ½ cup of powdered sugar, optional

Cooking Instructions:
1. Grease a metal dish that will fit into your Instant Pot.
2. In a medium bowl, mix together the flour, baking powder, and salt. Set 2 tbsp. aside.
3. Add the zest, sugar, and room temperature butter to mixer and beat until everything is combined.
4. Add the egg and vanilla to the mixer and combine. Working in batches in 1 cup at a time, add the flour mixture and buttermilk to the sugared butter in the stand mixer.
5. Incorporate everything and add another 1 cup at a time. Carefully take out the mixer bowl. Gently toss the blueberries with reserved 2 tbsp. of flour and fold into the batter.
6. Add 2/3 cup of water into the bottom of your Instant Pot and place the rack. Add half of batter into greased metal dish and place into the Instant Pot.
7. Select Manual, High Pressure for 30 minutes. When the timer beeps, do a quick pressure release. Carefully open the lid and take out the cake.
8. Mix together the juice from ½ a lemon with ½ cup of powdered sugar and pour over cake if desired.
9. Serve and enjoy!

Spanish Chorizo Breakfast Hash

Preparation time: 5 minutes
Cook time: 15 minutes
Total time: 20 minutes
Servings: 4

Ingredients:
- 6 large potatoes, peeled and diced
- 1 chorizo sausage, thinly sliced
- 4 slices of back bacon, sliced into chunks
- 1 medium onion, peeled and diced
- 250 g soft cheese
- 2 tablespoons of Greek yoghurt
- 1 tablespoon of garlic puree
- 1 tablespoon of olive oil
- 200 ml of vegetable stock
- 3 tablespoons of rosemary
- 3 tablespoons f basil
- A dash of salt
- A pinch of pepper

Cooking Instructions:
1. Add the onion, garlic and olive oil into the bottom of your Instant Pot.
2. Press the Sauté function and sauté until the onions have softened. Add the diced potatoes and sliced sausages.
3. Give everything a good stir and add a drop of little olive oil if desired. Add the sliced bacon. Add the seasoning and cook for a few more minutes.
4. Add the stock. Close and lock the lid in place and ensure that the valve is in sealing position. Select the Soup function to cook for 10 minutes.
5. When the timer beeps, do a natural pressure release for about 10 minutes. The potatoes will drain the stock water.
6. But if it hasn't, drain it in a sieve. In a mixing bowl, add a more herbs and mix in the soft cheese and Greek yoghurt.
7. Serve and enjoy!

Banana Oatmeal

Preparation time: 5 minutes
Cook time: 20 minutes
Total time: 25 minutes
Servings: 2

Ingredients:
- 1 cup of water
- 1 cup of milk (We used 1% fat milk)
- ½ cup of steel cut oats
- ¼ tsp. of cinnamon powder
- ½ of a large banana, mashed
- 1-2 tbsp. of brown sugar, adjust to taste
- Splash of vanilla extract
- Topping: peanut butter, sliced bananas and almonds/pecans

Cooking Instructions:
1. Spray your Instant Pot steel pot with a non-stick spray.
2. Add together the water, milk, steel cut oats, cinnamon powder. Add the mashed banana on top and do not stir.
3. Close and lock the lid in place and ensure that the valve is in sealing position. Select the Porridge function to cook for 15 minutes.
4. When the timer beeps, do a quick pressure release. Carefully open the lid and allow to cool for a couple of minutes.
5. Serve and enjoy!

Breakfast Quinoa

Servings: 6
Preparation time: 10 minutes
Cook time: 1 minute
Total time: 11 minutes

Ingredients:
- 1 ½ cups of uncooked quinoa, rinsed
- 2 ¼ cups of water
- 2 tbsp. of maple syrup
- ½ tsp. of vanilla
- ¼ tsp. of ground cinnamon
- Dash of salt
- Milk, fresh berries, sliced almonds, optional for topping

Cooking Instructions:
1. Add the quinoa, water, maple syrup, vanilla, cinnamon, and salt into the bottom of your Instant Pot.
2. Close and lock the lid in place. Select Manual, High Pressure for 1 minute.
3. When the timer beeps, do a natural pressure release for about 10 minutes, then quick release any remaining pressure.
4. Carefully open the lid and fluff the quinoa.
5. Serve warm with milk, berries, and sliced almonds.

Macaroni and Cheese

Preparation time: 10 minutes
Cook time: 6 minutes
Total time: 16 minutes

Ingredients:
- 2 cups of uncooked macaroni
- 2 cups of water
- ½ cup of evaporated milk
- 1 tablespoon of butter
- ½ teaspoon of salt
- 1 teaspoon of pepper or more to taste
- ½ cup of shredded cheddar cheese
- ½ cup of shredded smoked gouda cheese

Cooking Instructions:
1. Add the macaroni and water into the bottom of your Instant Pot.
2. Ensure that the noodles are submerged in water. Close and lock the lid in place. Select Manual, High Pressure for 6 minutes.
3. When the timer beeps, do a quick pressure release. Carefully remove the lid and dump in your cheeses, evaporated milk, salt, and butter.
4. Give everything a good mix for about 2 minutes or until a creamy/thick consistency is achieved. Sprinkle with pepper.
5. Serve and enjoy!

Spiced Apple Steel Cut Oats

Preparation time: 3 minutes
Cook time: 3 minutes
Total time: 6 minutes
Yield: 4
Ingredients:
- 1 1/3 cup of steel cut oats
- 4 cups of water
- 1 teaspoon of cinnamon
- ¼ teaspoon of ground nutmeg
- ¼ teaspoon of ground ginger
- ¼ teaspoon of all-spice
- 2 apples, chopped

Cooking Instructions:
1. Add all of the ingredients into the bottom of your Instant Pot.
2. Give everything a good stir to incorporate. Close and lock the lid in place and ensure that the valve is in sealing position.
3. Select Manual, High Pressure for 3 minutes. When the timer beeps, do a natural pressure release for about 10 minutes.
4. Carefully open the lid and spoon into a serving bowl. Top with your desired choice like maple syrup, grass-fed butter, and chopped pecans.
5. Serve and enjoy!

Fajita Breakfast Casserole

Preparation time: 10 minutes
Cook time: 2 minutes
Total time: 12 minutes
Servings: 2

Ingredients:
- ½ cup of onion, sliced
- 1 ½ cup of sliced bell peppers green, red, and orange
- 1 tablespoon of olive oil
- 4 eggs
- A dash of salt and pepper
- Cilantro avocado, and limes, optional for garnish

Cooking Instructions:
1. Press the Sauté button and add the olive. Add in the garlic, onions, and bell peppers to sauté them.
2. Sauté the ingredients for about 5 minutes until the onions and bell peppers are browned. Cancel the Sauté function.
3. Place the bell peppers and onions to a 2-quart soufflé pan that will fit into your Instant Pot. Lightly crack 4 eggs and place them on top of the peppers.
4. Sprinkle with salt and pepper and cover with a piece of aluminum foil. Make a foil sling with a large piece of foil folded into thirds.
5. Add the trivet into the bottom of your Instant Pot insert and pour 1 cup of water. Carefully lower the dish with the foil sling to sit on top of the trivet.
6. Close and lock the lid in place and ensure that the valve is in sealing position. Select Manual, High Pressure for 2 minutes.
7. When the timer beeps, do a quick pressure release. Carefully open the lid and lift out the pan from the Instant Pot. Top with avocados, cilantro, and sliced limes.
8. Serve and enjoy!

Chocolate Bircher Muesli

Preparation time: 5 minutes
Cook time: 15 minutes
Total time: 20 minutes
Servings: 2

Ingredients:
- 1 ½ cup of Greek yogurt
- Dollop of honey or maple syrup
- 1 tsp. of vanilla essence
- 1 cup of rolled oats organic
- 1 cup of milk
- 1 tbsp. of chia seeds
- Handful toasted almonds & chopped
- Fresh raspberries or your desired fruit
- ½ cup of orange juice
- 1 tbsp. of heaped cocoa powder
- Some dak chocolate chips / dark chopped chocolate

Cooking Instructions:
1. Blend together the chia seeds and milk for about 2 minutes and set aside.
2. Place the almonds in a pan, chop it and set aside too. In a medium bowl, add together the Greek yogurt, rolled oats, honey or maple syrup and vanilla essence.
3. Give everything a good mix and add the chia seeds mixture, cocoa powder, and orange juice.
4. Give everything a good mix and refrigerate for at least 10 minutes. When ready to serve, serve with raspberries, chopped toasted almonds and dark chocolate on top.
5. Serve and enjoy!

Blueberry Oatmeal

Preparation time: 5 minutes
Cook time: 30 minutes
Total time: 35 minutes
Servings: 6

Ingredients:
- 2 ¼ cups of whole oats
- ½ cup of brown sugar
- 14 oz. of canned coconut milk
- 3 cups of water
- 1 cup of blueberries frozen or fresh
- 1 tsp. of vanilla
- 1/8 tsp. of salt
- ¼ cup of gluten free flour blend

Cooking Instructions:
1. Add all of the ingredients into the bottom of your Instant Pot.
2. Close and lock the lid in place and ensure that the valve is in sealing position. Select the Bake function for 30 minutes.
3. When the timer beeps, do a quick pressure release. Carefully open the lid and spoon into a serving bowl.
4. Serve warm and enjoy!

Vanilla Apple Cinnamon Breakfast Quinoa

Preparation time: 10 minutes
Cook time: 1 minute
Total time: 11 minutes

Ingredients:
- 1 cup of quinoa
- 1.5 cup of water
- ¼ teaspoon of mineral salt
- 1 chopped apple
- 2 teaspoons of cinnamon
- ½ teaspoon of vanilla
- ¼ cup of gentle sweet

Cooking Instructions:
1. Place all the ingredients into the bottom of your Instant Pot and give everything a good stir.
2. Close and secure the lid in place and ensure that the valve is in sealing position. Select Manual, High Pressure for 1 minute.
3. When the timer beeps, do a natural pressure release for about 8 minutes. Carefully remove the lid and spoon into a serving bowl.
4. Serve and enjoy!

Chocolate Steel Cut Oats

Preparation time: 5 minutes
Cook time: 9 minutes
Total time: 14 minutes
Servings: 4

Ingredients:
- 1 cup / 176g / 6.2 ounces of steel cut oats
- 3 medium bananas
- 3 tbsp. of cocoa
- 3½ cups of water

Cooking Instructions:
1. Add together the oats, water and cocoa into the bottom of your Instant Pot.
2. Give everything a good stir. Mash the bananas with a fork until a puree them into smaller chunks.
3. Add pureed banana on top of the other ingredients and do not stir. Close and lock the lid in place and ensure that the valve is in sealing position.
4. Select Manual, High Pressure for 9 minutes. When the timer beeps, do a natural pressure release for about 10 minutes.
5. Carefully open the lid and stir the oatmeal. Allow to cool to thicken. Add more water or milk before serving.
6. Serve and enjoy!

Double Berry Oatmeal

Preparation time: 10 minutes
Cook time: 3 minutes
Total time: 13 minutes

Ingredients:
- 1 cup of steel cut oats
- ¼ cup of dried tart cherries
- ¼ cup of dried blueberries
- 3 cups of water
- Fresh blueberries (optional)
- Half & half (optional)

Cooking Instructions:
1. Add the oatmeal, dried cherries, dried blueberries and water into the bottom of your Instant Pot.
2. Close and lock the lid in place and ensure that the valve is in sealing position. Select Manual, High Pressure for 3 minutes.
3. When the timer beeps, do a natural pressure release for about 7 minutes, then quick release any remaining pressure.
4. Carefully remove the lid and give the oatmeal a good stir. Allow the oatmeal to cool as it absorbs the remaining cooking liquid to thicken.
5. Serve topped with more fresh blueberries or even a touch of half & half!

INSTANT POT SOUP & STEW RECIPES

Italian Wedding Soup

Preparation time: 20 minutes
Cook time: 4 minutes
Total time: 24 minutes
Servings: 6

Ingredients:
- 12 meatballs (sausage)
- 40 ounces of chicken broth
- 1 onion, diced
- 3 carrots, diced
- 1 bunch escarole (use 2 c. leaves)
- ½ cup of Pastini
- ¼ teaspoon of basil dried

Cooking Instructions:
1. Add a little tablespoon of olive oil into your Instant Pot. Press the Sauté function, set to low, and add your meatballs.
2. Sauté the outsides if you're cooking using your own fresh meatballs. Defrost the meatballs if using frozen and add to the pot.
3. Add the onions and cook for a couple of minutes to soften onions slightly. Press the Cancel function.
4. Add in your chicken stock, diced carrots, basil, and Pastini noodles. Close and lock the lid in place and ensure that the valve is in sealing position.
5. Select Manual, High Pressure for 4 minutes. When the timer beeps, do a quick pressure release. Carefully open the lid and add the escarole.
6. Give everything a good stir so leaves are submerged. Press the Sauté function, low and let to bubble for about 2-3 minutes to soften the escarole.
7. Serve and enjoy!

Mexican Chicken Stew

Preparation time: 10 minutes
Cook time: 23 minutes
Total time: 32 minutes
Serves: 8

Ingredients:
- 3 lbs. of chicken pieces, skinned
- 2 cups of thinly sliced onion
- ¾ tsp. of salt
- ½ tsp. of coarsely ground black pepper
- 3 (14.5-oz.) cans fat-free, lower-sodium chicken broth
- 4 garlic cloves, crushed
- 3 bell peppers, seeded and chopped
- 1 bay leaf
- 1 (15-oz.) can golden or white hominy, drained
- 2 tbsp. of ground guajillo chile powder
- 1 ½ tsp. of dried oregano
- ½ cup of roasted unsalted pumpkinseed kernels
- ¼ cup of chopped fresh cilantro
- ¼ cup of sliced radishes
- ¼ cup of sliced scallions
- ½ cup of crumbled queso fresco cheese

Cooking Instructions:
1. Add the first 8 ingredients into the bottom of your Instant Pot. Close and secure the lid in place.
2. Select Manual, High Pressure for 23 minutes. When the timer beeps, do a quick pressure release. Carefully open the lid.
3. Lift out the chicken from broth mixture and allow to cool. Remove the chicken from bones; cut chicken into bite-sized pieces.
4. Discard the bones. Strain stock through a sieve over a bowl and remove the solids. Add the inner pot to into the Instant Pot and place the stock into the inner pot.
5. Add in chicken, hominy, chile powder, and oregano. Allow to sit for about 5 minutes. Drain the fat from surface of broth; discard.
6. Ladle the stew into 8 individual bowls and top each bowl with pumpkin-seed kernels, cilantro, radishes, scallions, and queso fresco cheese.
7. Serve and enjoy!

Minestrone Soup

Preparation time: 10 minutes
Cook time: 4 minutes
Total time: 14 minutes
Servings: 8

Ingredients:
- 1 can of kidney beans, drained
- 1 can of garbanzo beans, drained
- 32 ounces of chicken broth
- ½ onion, sliced or diced
- 2 stalks celery, diced
- 3 carrots, thinly sliced
- 1 small zucchini, cut into dials
- 1.5 cup of petite diced tomatoes
- 1 cup of uncooked shell noodles

Cooking Instructions:
1. First, dice all the vegetables and add them into the bottom of your Instant Pot.
2. Add the chicken broth and uncooked noodles. Give everything a good stir and add any herbs/spices you'd desire.
3. Close and lock the lid in place and ensure that the valve is in sealing position. Select Manual, High Pressure for 3 minutes.
4. When the timer beeps, do a quick pressure release. Carefully remove the lid and stir.
5. Serve topped with shredded parmesan and parsley if desired.

Brunswick Stew

Preparation time: 10 minutes
Cook time: 25 minutes
Total time: 35 minutes
Serves: 8

Ingredients:
- 1 (26.5 ounces) pkg. chopped tomatoes (like Pomì)
- 1 ¼ lb. of Yukon Gold potatoes (about 2 large potatoes), cut into 1-in. cubes
- 2 cups of chopped Vidalia onion
- ½ cup of packed light brown sugar
- 6 tbsp. of Worcestershire sauce
- ¼ cup of apple cider vinegar
- ¼ cup of Dijon mustard
- 2 tbsp. of chopped fresh thyme
- 1 tbsp. of kosher salt
- 1 tbsp. of tomato paste
- 2 tsp. of unsweetened cocoa
- ¼ tsp. of crushed red pepper
- 1 (4 pounds) whole chicken
- 2 cups of frozen lima beans
- 2 cups of fresh or frozen corn kernels (about 4 ears)
- ½ tsp. of black pepper
- 1/3 cup of thinly sliced scallions (about 2 scallions)

Cooking Instructions:
1. In your Instant Pot, add together the tomatoes, potatoes, onion, and Worcestershire sauce.
2. Add the vinegar, mustard, thyme, salt, tomato paste, cocoa, and red pepper and give everything a good stir.
3. Add the chicken on top of tomato mixture. Close and lock the lid in place and ensure that the valve is in sealing position.
4. Select Manual, High Pressure for 25 minutes. When the timer beeps, do a quick pressure release.
5. Carefully open the lid and transfer the chicken to a bow. Allow the chicken to cool for about 15 minutes.
6. Give the tomato mixture a good stir and reduce heat to medium to maintain a low simmer. Stir in lima beans, corn, and black pepper.
7. Cook the vegetables for about 2 minutes. When the chicken has cooled, remove and discard the chicken skin.
8. Shred the chicken with two forks and remove the bones. Discard bones, and stir chicken meat and scallions into tomato mixture and give everything a good stir.
9. Serve immediately and enjoy!

Tomato Basil Soup

Preparation time: 10 minutes
Cook time: 9 minutes
Total time: 19 minutes
Servings: 6

Ingredients:
- 29 ounces of tomato sauce
- 8 basil leaves fresh, or 1 tablespoon of dried basil
- 1 tablespoon of garlic, minced
- 1 cup of heavy whipping cream
- 1-2 cup of tortellini, optional
- ½ onion, diced
- 1 teaspoon of pepper
- ½ cup of parmesan cheese, optional
- A pinch of taste

Cooking Instructions:
1. Press the Sauté function on your Instant Pot and add a little drop of olive oil.
2. Add the diced onions and garlic. Sauté for a couple of minutes until onions starts to soften. Press the Cancel function.
3. Add the half of the basil leaves and can of tomato sauce and give everything a good stir. Close and lock the lid in place and ensure that the valve is in sealing position.
4. Select Manual, High Pressure for 2 minutes. When the timer beeps, do a quick pressure release. Press the Sauté function and add the stuffed tortellini noodles.
5. Sauté for about 5 minutes stirring frequently, until tortellini's are as tender. Add in whipping cream and give everything a good stir.
6. Cook for additional 2 minutes and stir again. Serve topped with additional basil, salt and/ or parmesan cheese if desired.

Cuban Shredded Beef Stew

Preparation time: 20 minutes
Cook time: 40 minutes
Total time: 1 hour
Serves: 6-8

Ingredients:
- 1 tbsp. of olive oil
- 2 pounds of beef flank steak
- A pinch of salt
- Pepper to taste
- 1 medium onion, sliced
- 4-5 cloves garlic, minced
- 1 cup of beef or chicken broth
- 1 15 ounces can diced tomatoes
- 2 cups of sliced mild/sweet peppers (such as cubanelles)
- ½ tsp. of dried oregano
- 1 tsp. of ground cumin
- 1 bay leaf
- ½ - 1 tsp. of Goya Sazon or Adobo seasoning
- ½ cup f chopped fresh parsley
- 2 tbsp. of vinegar (such as white wine, distilled, apple cider)
- ½ cup of chopped green olives

Cooking Instructions:
1. Generously season the flank steak with salt and pepper on both sides. Set your Instant Pot to Sauté function and add the olive oil.
2. Once the oil is hot, add the meat. Sauté the meat on both sides and transfer to a bowl. Add the onions and garlic.
3. Cook the contents over medium sauté heat, stirring frequently, until the onions start to soften. Add the broth and scrape up any browned bits stuck to the bottom of the pot.
4. Add the canned tomatoes, sliced peppers, oregano, cumin, and bay leaf (and seasoning blend, if desired). Give everything a good stir to combine.
5. Nestle the browned flank steak into the stew. Close and lock the lid in place and ensure that the valve is in sealing position.
6. Select Manual, High Pressure for 40 minutes. When the timer beeps, do a natural pressure release for about 10 minutes.
7. Carefully remove the lid and transfer the meat to a bowl. Shred the meat with two forks. Discard the bay leaf.
8. Add in the parsley, vinegar and green olives. Season to taste, and give everything a good mix.
9. Serve with rice and enjoy!

Broccoli Cheese Soup

Preparation time: 15 minutes
Cook time: 30 minutes
Total time: 45 minutes
Servings: 6

Ingredients:
- 2 heads broccoli, cut into small, bite size pieces
- 1 carrot, diced
- 1 stalk celery, diced
- ½ onion, diced
- 2 cups of heavy cream
- 2 tablespoons of flour or cornstarch
- 8 ounces of cheese shredded or cut into small chunks
- 3 cups of vegetable broth or water

Cooking Instructions:
1. Add all diced vegetables into the bottom of your Instant Pot.
2. Sprinkle the diced vegetables with shredded cheese on top.
3. In a medium bowl, whisk together the vegetable broth or water, heavy cream and flour or cornstarch until there are no clumps remaining.
4. Add the mixture on top of everything inside your Instant Pot. Close and lock the lid in place and ensure that the valve is in sealing position.
5. Select the Soup function to cook for 30 minutes. When the timer beeps, do a quick pressure release. Carefully remove the lid and stir.
6. Serve, topped with added shredded cheese if desired.

Spicy Ethiopian Stew

Preparation time: 10 minutes
Cook time: 15 minutes
Total time: 25 minutes
Yield: 6

Ingredients:
- 1½ cups of dried lentils
- 3 garlic cloves, minced
- 3 tbsp. of tomato paste
- 3-5 tsp. of Berbere Spice
- 5 cups of vegetable broth
- 1 yellow onion, chopped
- 2 ½ cups of butternut squash, cut into chunks
- ½ tsp. of sea salt
- ½ tbsp. of maple syrup
- 2 tbsp. of pureed ginger
- 1/2 (10 oz.) bag chopped frozen spinach

Cooking Instructions:
1. Add all the ingredients into the bottom of your Instant Pot.
2. Close and lock the lid in place and ensure that the valve is in sealing position.
3. Select Manual, High Pressure for 15 minutes. When the timer beeps, do a natural pressure release.
4. Carefully remove the lid and give everything a good stir.
5. Serve and enjoy!

Cheeseburger Soup

Preparation time: 10 minutes
Cook time: 3 minutes
Total time: 13 minutes
Servings: 5

Ingredients:
- 1 pound of hamburger or ground sausage if you desire
- ½ onion, diced
- 2 stalks celery, sliced
- 8 pieces of bacon, diced
- 2 tablespoons of butter
- 1 teaspoon of seasoned salt
- 1 teaspoon of garlic powder
- 3 cups of chicken broth or beef broth
- 2 cups of cheese
- ½ cup of heavy cream
- 3 tablespoons of cornstarch
- ½ cup of sour cream, optional for topping

Cooking Instructions:
1. Press the Sauté function on your Instant Pot and add the butter to melt.
2. Add the ground beef and diced onions. Sauté the contents until the ground beef has cooked through. Add the diced bacon and diced celery into the pot.
3. Press the Cancel function. Add the seasoned salt and garlic powder and give everything a good stir. Pour in chicken or beef broth if desired and stir again.
4. Close and lock the lid in place and ensure that the valve is in sealing position. Select Manual, High Pressure for 3 minutes.
5. When the timer beeps, do a quick pressure release. Press the Cancel function. Turn on the Sauté function, normal, and add the heavy cream.
6. Add the 1 ½ cup of your desired cheese and stir to melt the cheese. Add some of the hot cooking liquid to a medium bowl with cornstarch and whisk together.
7. Pour the mixture into the Instant Pot and give everything a good stir to thicken. Press the Cancel function.
8. Add the rest of the ½ cup of cheese and give everything a good stir. Serve, topped with more shredded cheese and chives/green onions or a dollop of sour cream.
9. Serve immediately and enjoy!

Andouille Sausage Stew

Preparation time: 10 minutes
Cook time: 20 minutes
Total time: 30 minutes
Serves: 6

Ingredients:
- 1 lb. of uncooked Pork Andouille Sausage, crumbled
- 1 medium onion, halved and thinly sliced
- ½ lb. of grape or cherry tomatoes
- 1 ½ lb. of Yukon Gold potatoes, peeled and cut into 1" pieces
- ¾ lb. of collard greens, stems removed and thinly sliced
- 1 cup of chicken broth
- 1 tsp. of kosher salt
- 20 - 25 turns of freshly ground black pepper
- ½ medium lemon, freshly squeezed

Cooking Instructions:
1. Press the Sauté function on your Instant Pot and add the andouille sausage.
2. Cook the sausage for about 5 to 8 minutes, stirring occasionally. Add the sliced onions and tomatoes.
3. Give everything a good mix and cook for another 3 to 4 minutes. Add the potatoes, collard greens and broth along with salt and pepper.
4. Close and lock the lid in place and ensure that the valve is in sealing position. Select Manual, High Pressure for 10 minutes.
5. When the timer beeps, do a quick pressure release. Carefully remove the lid and add the fresh lemon juice. Season with salt and pepper to taste.
6. Serve and enjoy!

Potato Leek Soup

Preparation time: 10 minutes
Cook time: 12 minutes
Total time: 22 minutes
Servings: 8

Ingredients:
- 2 tablespoons of butter or olive oil
- 2 large leek white and pale green parts, sliced thinly
- 4 medium potatoes, peeled and diced
- 6 cups of veggie broth
- Salt and pepper to taste
- Fresh parsley to garnish

Cooking Instructions:
1. Press the Sauté function on your Instant Pot and add the butter.
2. Add the leeks and sauté until they soften. Add in the potatoes and broth. Close and lock the lid in place and ensure that the valve is in sealing position.
3. Select Manual, High Pressure for 12 minutes. When the timer beeps, do a quick pressure release.
4. Carefully remove the lid and season with salt and pepper to taste. Add the parsley and give everything a good stir.
5. Serve and enjoy!

Hoppin' John Stew

Preparation time: 20 minutes
Cook time: 30 minutes
Total time: 50 minutes
Serves: 4-6

Ingredients:
- 1 medium onion, chopped
- 4 stalks of celery, chopped
- 4 cloves fresh garlic, minced
- 1 stalk rosemary, tough stem removed, finely chopped
- ½ lb. of dried black-eyed peas
- ½ cup of uncooked wild rice, rinsed
- 1 15 oz. can of low or no-sodium diced tomatoes
- 1 15 oz. can of low or no-sodium fire roasted tomatoes
- 2 cups of chopped kale
- 4 cups of no or low sodium vegetable broth
- 1-3 cups of water or enough to cover the beans
- ½ cup of nutritional yeast
- ¼ cup of no or low sodium vegetable soup base (We used Dr. Fuhrman's VegiZest)

Cooking Instructions:
1. Turn on the Sauté button, high and add the onion.
2. Add the celery and cook until it starts to turn translucent. Add the garlic and rosemary and stir for about 1 to 2 minutes.
3. Press the Cancel/Keep Warm function. Add the remaining ingredients and ensure that the ingredients are covered with liquid.
4. Close and lock the lid in place and ensure that the valve is in sealing position. Press the Beans/Chili button and set timer to 25 minutes.
5. When the timer beeps, do a natural pressure release for about 15 minutes. Carefully open the lid and stir.
6. Serve and enjoy!

French Onion Soup

Preparation time: 10 minutes
Cook time: 3 minutes
Total time: 13 minutes
Servings: 4

Ingredients:
- 3 onions, sliced
- 3 tablespoons of butter
- ¾ teaspoon of salt
- 2 tablespoons of Worchester shire sauce
- ¾ teaspoon of thyme
- 32 ounces of beef broth
- ¾ cup of mozzarella cheese shredded, for top
- 1 loaf French bread day old, sliced
- ¼ cup of green onions diced, optional

Cooking Instructions:
1. Press the Sauté button on your Instant Pot and add the butter to melt.
2. Add the onions and cook until softened. Add the sliced onions, salt, Worchester shire sauce, thyme and beef broth.
3. Close and lock the lid in place and ensure that the valve is in sealing position. Select Manual, High Pressure for 3 minutes.
4. When the timer beeps, do a quick pressure release. Carefully open the lid and stir.
5. Serve with bread on the side, or melt cheese on slices of French bread.

Irish Stew

Preparation time: 10 minutes
Cook time: 20 minutes
Total time: 30 minutes

Ingredients:
- 1.5 cup of beef broth (Mixed beef and vegetable broth)
- 1.5 cup of Guinness or other dark stout
- 2 lb. boneless lamb or stew beef, trim off extra fat and cube into about 1 inch pieces
- 12 small red potatoes, rinsed and cut in half or quarters
- 14 oz. can of diced tomatoes
- 1 chopped onion
- 3-4 carrots, sliced into half inch rounds
- 2-3 parsnips, sliced into half inch rounds
- 1-2 small turnips, sliced in half and into half inch strips
- 1-2 bay leaves
- 1 tsp. of salt
- 1 tsp. of black pepper
- 1 tsp. of minced garlic (fresh or jarred)
- 4 tbsp. of all-purpose flour
- 16 oz. of bag frozen peas
- ¼ cup of chopped fresh parsley

Cooking Instructions:
1. Season the lamb cubes or stew beef with salt, pepper and garlic. Mix well on both sides.
2. Keep the lamb cubes aside to come to room temperature. Add the broth, stout or extra broth into the bottom of your Instant Pot.
3. Add the lamb (or stew beef), potatoes, carrots, onion, parsnips, turnips, and tomatoes into the pot. Give everything a good mix with a large spoon.
4. Add the bay leaves. Close and lock the lid in place and ensure that the valve is in sealing position. Select Manual, High Pressure for 20 minutes.
5. When the timer beeps, do a natural pressure release for about 10 minutes, then quick release any remaining pressure.
6. Carefully open the lid and stir. Press the Sauté function and bring the stew to a boil. Add the flour and 1.2 cup of water into a covered jar and shake to combine the content.
7. Pour the mixture into the stew in the Instant Pot and give everything a good stir until the stew thickens. Add in bag of frozen peas and chopped parsley before serving.
8. Serve immediately and enjoy!

Chicken Noodle Soup

Preparation time: 10 minutes
Cook time: 3 minutes
Total time: 13 minutes
Servings: 5

Ingredients:
- 2 chicken breasts cubed,, bite size, boneless skinless
- 2 tablespoons of olive oil
- ¼ teaspoon of salt
- Pepper, to taste
- 2 carrots, sliced thin
- 2 stalks celery, sliced
- ¼ onion, diced
- 48 oz. of chicken broth or half chicken, cut into bite size chunks
- 2 cup of egg noodles uncooked
- ¼ teaspoon of basil
- ¼ teaspoon of oregano

Cooking Instructions:
1. Set your Instant Pot on sauté low and add the olive oil.
2. Add the chicken, celery, onions, and carrots. Sauté the ingredients until the chicken are a bit cooked on outside and veggies soften just slightly.
3. Press the Cancel function. Add the chicken broth, uncooked noodles, salt, pepper, and spices if desired into the bottom of your Instant Pot.
4. Close and lock the lid in place and ensure that the valve is in sealing position. Select Manual, High Pressure for 3 minutes.
5. When the timer beeps, do a natural pressure release for about 10 minutes. Carefully remove the lid and stir.
6. Serve and enjoy!

Cheddar Broccoli & Potato Soup

Preparation time: 10 minutes
Cook time: 15 minutes
Total time: 25 minutes
Servings: 4-6

Ingredients:
- 2 tablespoons of butter
- 2 cloves garlic, crushed
- 1 medium sized broccoli head, broken into large florets
- 2 pounds of Yukon Gold Potatoes, peeled and cut into bite chunks
- 4 cups of vegetable or chicken broth
- Salt to taste
- Pepper to taste
- 1 cup of half and half
- 1 cup of shredded cheddar cheese
- 6 slices of bacon (optional)
- Chopped green onion or chives for garnish

Cooking Instructions:
1. Press the Sauté button on your Instant Pot and add the butter.
2. Add the crushed garlic and cook for about 1 minute, or until garlic starts to brown. Add the broccoli, potatoes, and broth.
3. Add extra salt and pepper. Close and lock the lid in place and ensure that the valve is in sealing position. Select Manual, High Pressure for 5 minutes.
4. When the timer beeps, do a natural pressure release for about 10 minutes, then quick release any remaining pressure.
5. If using bacon, place it in a microwave or cook until desired your desire crispiness is achieved. Keep aside to cool.
6. Carefully open the lid and add the half and half and ½ cup of cheddar cheese. Pour the soup in an immersion blender and blend until smooth.
7. Add more broth if your desire a thinner soup. Season with salt and pepper to taste.
8. Serve hot with rest of the cheddar and bacon (if using).

Italian Beef Stew

Preparation time: 10 minutes
Cook time: 35 minutes
Total time: 45 minutes
Servings: 6-8

Ingredients:
- 3 pounds of beef stew meat OR 2 pounds of ground beef, browned.
- 1 onion, diced
- 4 carrots, sliced
- 8 ounces of fresh baby portabella mushrooms, sliced (optional)
- 24 ounces of beef broth
- 15 ounces can of diced tomatoes
- 3 tablespoons of flour
- 1 teaspoon of dried basil leaves
- 1 teaspoon of dried thyme leaves
- 1 teaspoon of salt
- 1 teaspoon of pepper Dried parsley

Cooking Instructions:
1. Press the Sauté function on your Instant Pot and add the meat.
2. Drain the grease if using ground beef. Add the carrots, broth, flour, basil, thyme, salt, pepper and diced tomatoes into the bottom of your Instant Pot.
3. Give everything a good stir. Close and lock the lid in place and ensure that the valve is in sealing position.
4. Select Manual, High Pressure for 35 minutes. When the timer beeps, do a quick pressure release. Carefully open the lid and stir in mushrooms.
5. Serve and enjoy!

Swiss Chard Stem Soup

Ingredients:
- 2 tbsp. of olive oil
- 8 cups of Swiss Chard Stems, diced
- 3 Leeks, green and white, diced
- Celeriac, peeled and diced
- Potato, peeled and diced
- 1.5 cups of chicken stock
- 1 cup of coconut milk (almond/coconut milk.)
- Salt to taste
- Pepper to taste

Cooking Instructions:
1. Press the Sauté function on your Instant Pot and add 2 tbsp. of oil. Add the leeks and cook until soft.
2. Add the diced Swiss chard, cooked leeks, celeriac, potato, chicken stock and coconut milk. Add salt and pepper.
3. Close and lock the lid in place and ensure that the valve is in sealing position. Press the "Soup" button and it will cook automatically.
4. When the timer beeps, do a quick pressure release. Carefully remove the lid and blend the soup with an immersion blender.
5. Serve and enjoy!

Apple Spice Beef Stew

Preparation time: 10 minutes
Cook time: 22 minutes
Total time: 32 minutes
Serves: 5-6

Ingredients:

- 1 kilogram grass fed beef, cut into bite size chunks
- 2 apples, chopped
- 1 medium white onion, chopped
- 3 or 4 large carrots, bite size chunks
- 2 tablespoons of garlic flakes OR 1 1/2 tablespoon of powder
- 1 teaspoon of cinnamon powder
- ¼ teaspoon of cloves powder
- 1 tablespoon of dried Oregano
- 1 teaspoon of sea salt
- 1 ½ cup of homemade broth

Cooking Instructions:

1. Press the Sauté function on your Instant Pot and add 1 tablespoon of olive oil.
2. Add the onion and meat and sauté for about 6 minutes or until the meat is no longer pink.
3. Add the spices and cook for additional 3 minutes. Add the rest of the ingredients.
4. Close and lock the lid in place and ensure that the valve is in sealing position.
5. Select Manual, High Pressure for 22 minutes. When the timer beeps, do a quick pressure release. Carefully open the lid and stir.
6. Serve alongside a baked sweet potato if desired and enjoy!

Spanish Infused Chicken Stew

Preparation time: 10 minutes
Cook time: 3 hours
Total time: 3 hours 10 minutes

Ingredients:
- 4 chicken breasts, cut into chunks
- 4 cloves of garlic, minced
- ½ cooking chorizo, chopped
- 2 carrots, chopped
- 2 courgettes, chopped
- 2 leeks, chopped
- 3 red skinned potatoes, scrubbed and chopped in half
- 1 can of cannellini beans
- 1 handful of parsley, chopped
- A small handful of oregano, chopped
- 1 glass of fino sherry or dry white wine
- A pinch of smoked paprika
- A few strands of saffron
- Salt to taste
- Pepper to taste
- Chicken stock, enough to cover

Cooking Instructions:
1. Prepare the vegetables and add them into the bottom of your Instant Pot.
2. Add a few drops of oil in a sauté pan and add the garlic. Add the chicken and chorizo and sauté until the chicken is browned.
3. Add the chicken, chorizo and garlic mixture into the bottom of your Instant Pot. Give everything a good stir.
4. Cook the stock and add the herbs, spices and seasonings. Pour chicken stock enough to cover the contents.
5. Close and lock the lid in place and ensure that the valve is in sealing position. Select the Slow cook function and set to cook for 3 hours.
6. When the timer beeps, do a quick pressure release. Carefully open the lid and adjust the seasoning.
7. Serve with crusty bread or rice.

Red Pepper Tomato Soup

Preparation time: 10 minutes
Cook time: 5 minutes
Total time: 15 minutes

Ingredients:
- 1 tbsp. of butter
- 1 tbsp. of oil
- 2 white onions, diced
- 8 red bell peppers, diced
- 8 cloves garlic, minced
- 4 medium tomatoes (or 2 canned fire roasted tomatoes)
- 2 tsp. of herbes de provence
- ½ tsp. of paprika
- ¼ tsp. of cayenne pepper
- 2-3 cups of bone or vegetable broth
- ½ tsp. of salt
- ½ tsp. of pepper
- Parsley or Cilantro for garnish

Cooking Instructions:
1. Press the Sauté function on your Instant Pot and add the butter and oil.
2. Add the diced onions and sauté for a couple of minutes until they soften. Add the garlic, diced red peppers, and diced tomatoes into the bottom of your Instant Pot.
3. Add the herbes de provence, paprika, cayenne pepper, salt, and pepper. Give everything a good stir and let to cook for about 2 to 3 minutes.
4. Add 2 cups of broth and give everything a good stir. Close and lock the lid in place and ensure that the valve is in sealing position.
5. Select Manual, High Pressure for 5 minutes. When the timer beeps, do a quick pressure release. Carefully open the lid and blend the soup with an immersion blender.
6. Add rest of the broth to achieve your desired consistency. Adjust the seasoning with more salt and pepper to taste.
7. Serve and enjoy!

INSTANT POT FISH & SEAFOOD RECIPES

Brazilian Fish Stew

Preparation time: 15 minutes
Cook time: 40 minutes
Total time: 55 minutes
Servings: 5

Ingredients:
Stew Base Ingredients:
- 1 onion, diced
- 1 red bell pepper, sliced
- 5 cloves garlic, minced
- 14 oz. canned crushed tomatoes
- 8 oz. seafood or fish broth
- 6 oz. canned full-fat coconut milk
- 2 tbsp. of coconut oil
- 1 tbsp. of ground cumin
- 1 tbsp. of smoked paprika
- 1 tsp. of salt
- ½ tsp. of black pepper
- ¼ - ½ tsp. of ground cayenne

For Finishing:
- 1 ½ lb. of firm white fish like cod or halibut
- 2 tbsp. of coconut oil
- 1 tbsp. of lime juice
- 1 tbsp. of chopped fresh cilantro or parsley

Cooking Instructions:
1. Place all the stew base ingredients into the bottom of your Instant Pot and give everything a good stir until well-mixed.
2. Close and lock the lid in place and ensure that the valve is in sealing position. Select Manual, High Pressure 10 minutes.
3. When the timer beeps, do a natural pressure release for about 10 minutes. Carefully remove the lid and stir.
4. Press the Sauté function and allow the stew boil for 10 minutes to thicken the sauce, stirring frequently. Prepare the fish while the stew is boiling.
5. Remove the skin and discard bones from the fish. If the fish, pat dry with paper towels and cut into 1-inch pieces. Stir in fish when the stew has thickened.
6. Cook for about 5 minutes. Press the Cancel function. Stir in coconut oil and lime juice and give everything a good until combined.
7. Serve topped with chopped cilantro or parsley.

Salmon Croquettes

Preparation time: 10 minutes
Cook time: 3 minutes
Total time: 13 minutes
Servings: 2

Ingredients:
- 2 salmon filets
- ¼ cup of chopped onion
- 2 stalks green onion, chopped
- 1 egg
- Course Panko
- A pinch of salt
- A pinch of pepper
- 2 tbsp. of cooking oil

Cooking Instructions:
1. Pour 1 cup of water into the bottom of your Instant Pot and place the trivet in with the fish on top.
2. Generously season the fish with salt and pepper and add the fish into your pot. Close and lock the lid in place and ensure that the valve is in sealing position.
3. Select Manual, High Pressure for 3 minutes. When the timer beeps, do a quick pressure release. Carefully open the lid and remove the fish.
4. Allow the fish to cool for a couple of minutes. Break up the filets in a bowl and add the egg, yellow onion and green onion.
5. Add a ½ cup of Panko and give everything a good mix with your hands. Divide the mixture into 1/3 cup portions and form into patties with your hands.
6. Heat a large skillet over medium heat and add the oil. Add the patties into the skillet and cook until golden brown. Flip the patties and brown the other side.
7. Serve and enjoy!

Fish Coconut Curry

Preparation time: 10 minutes
Cook time: 10 minutes
Total time: 20 minutes
Servings: 4

Ingredients:
- 1 pound of Tilapia filets, cut in 2 inch pieces
- 1 tbsp. of olive oil
- ½ tsp. of mustard seeds
- 12 ounces coconut milk (1 can)
- 1 tbsp. of ginger-garlic paste : ½ inch ginger + 3 cloves garlic, crushed or ground
- 10 curry leaves or 2-3 kaffir lime leaves
- ½ medium onion, sliced
- ½ green pepper, sliced
- ½ orange pepper or yellow pepper, sliced
- 1 tsp. of salt
- ½ tsp. of turmeric powder
- ½ tsp. of red chili powder
- 2 tsp. of coriander powder
- 1 tsp. of cumin powder
- 1 tsp. of Garam masala
- 3 sprigs of cilantro
- 8 mint leaves, optional
- ½ tsp. of lime juice

Cooking Instructions:
1. In a mini-food processor, chop the ginger-garlic. Press the Sauté function on your Instant Pot and add the oil.
2. Add the mustard seeds. When the mustard seeds starts to splutter, add curry leaves and ginger-garlic paste and cook for about 30 seconds.
3. Add the sliced onions and bell peppers and cook for additional 30 seconds. Add all the spices and give everything a good stir.
4. Sauté for additional 30 seconds. Add the coconut milk and give everything a good mix. Bring the pot to a boil for 1 minute.
5. Add the Tilapia, a few cilantro sprigs and stir again to coat with coconut milk. Close and lock the lid in place and ensure that the valve is in sealing position.
6. Select Manual, High Pressure for 3 minutes. When the timer beeps, do a quick pressure release. Finish the curry with a light squeeze of lime.
7. Serve with brown rice/white rice or a slice of toasted baguette and enjoy!

Lemon Dill Salmon

Preparation time: 3 minutes
Cook time: 5 minutes
Total time: 8 minutes
Servings: 2

Ingredients:
- 2 salmon filets (1 inch thick, 3 oz.)
- 1 teaspoon of fresh dill chopped
- ½ teaspoon of salt
- ¼ teaspoon of pepper
- 1 cup of water
- 2 tablespoons of lemon juice
- ½ lemon, sliced

Cooking Instructions:
1. Generously season the salmon with dill, salt, and pepper.
2. Pour 1 cup of water into the bottom of your Instant Pot and place the steam rack. Arrange the salmon on steam rack, skin side down.
3. Squeeze the lemon juice over filets and add the lemon slices on top. Close and lock the lid in place and ensure that the valve in sealing position.
4. Select the Steam function and set to cook for 5 minutes. When the timer beeps, do a quick pressure release.
5. Ensure that the meat read at least 145°F with a meat thermometer.
6. Serve with additional dill and lemon slices.

Steamed Alaskan Crab Legs

- 2-3 lb. of frozen crab legs
- 1 cup of water
- ½ tbsp. of salt
- Melted butter

Cooking Instructions:
1. Pour 1 cup of water and salt into the bottom of your Instant Pot.
2. Place the steamer basket and add the half of the Alaskan King Crab Legs.
3. Close and lock the lid in place and ensure that the valve is in sealing position. Select Manual, High Pressure for 4 minutes.
4. When the timer beeps, do a quick pressure release. Carefully remove the lid. Remove the crab legs and serve with melted butter.
5. Repeat the same procedure with the remaining half of crab legs.

Manhattan Clam Chowder

Preparation time: 10 minutes
Cook time: 5 minutes
Total time: 15 minutes

Ingredients:
- 2 tablespoons of salted butter
- 1 medium onion, minced
- 2 celery stalks, sliced and finely chopped
- 1 pound of Idaho/Russet potatoes, peeled and diced
- 4 ounces of diced pancetta, optional
- 1 cup of clam or vegetable or chicken broth (We used 1 teaspoon of Clam Better Than Bouillon + 1 cup of water)
- 28 ounces can of crushed tomatoes
- 3 (6.5 ounces) cans of chopped clams, separating and reserve the clam juice
- ½ teaspoon of seasoned salt
- ½ teaspoon of Old Bay seasoning
- ½ teaspoon of black pepper
- 1/8 – ½ teaspoon of Zatarain's Concentrated Crab & Shrimp Boil, optional
- Oyster Crackers, for topping

Cooking Instructions:
1. Press the "Sauté" function in your Instant Pot and add the butter to melt. Add the onion, and celery and stir constantly for about 2-3 minutes until softened.
2. Add the diced pancetta if desired and give everything a good stir for additional 2-3 minutes, deglazing to remove any stuck bits from the bottom of the pot.
3. Add the clam or vegetable or chicken broth if desired and scrape any browned bit that's stuck to the bottom of the pot.
4. Add the crushed tomatoes, clam juice, seasoned salt, Old Bay, black pepper, Zatarain's, leafy tops from the celery and potatoes.
5. Give everything a good stir. Close and lock the lid in place and ensure that the valve is in sealing position. Select Manual, High Pressure for 5 minutes.
6. When the timer beeps, do a quick pressure release. Carefully remove the lid and stir in the reserved clams. Simmer for about 2 minutes to thicken.
7. Serve, topped with some oyster crackers, if desired and enjoy!

Lemon Scented Fish Broth

Preparation time: 10 minutes
Cook time: 30 minutes
Total time: 40 minutes
Serves: 2

Ingredients:
- 3 salmon heads and 1 tail, rinsed under running water and remove the fish gills
- 2 tbsp. of olive oil
- 1 onion, chopped
- 1 carrot, peeled and chopped
- ½ leek, chopped
- 1 celery stalk, chopped
- 3 stalks parsley
- 1 bay leaf
- 1 sprig of thyme
- 1 shard of lemon zest, removed from the lemon
- 60mls (4 tbsp.) of apple cider vinegar
- 1½ tsp. of sea salt

Cooking Instructions:
1. Press the Sauté button on your Instant Pot and add the olive oil. Cook the fish for about 2.
2. Add the remaining ingredients, and cook for additional 2 minutes. Deglaze the pot to remove any browned bits stuck to the bottom of the pot.
3. Pour 3½ liter of water into the bottom of your Instant Pot. Secure the lid in place and ensure that the valve is in sealing position.
4. Select Manual, High Pressure for 10 minutes. When the timer beeps, do a natural pressure release for about 15 minutes.
5. Carefully remove the lid and remove all the fish and vegetables from the pot. Use a fine sieve to drain the broth.
6. Pour the broth into mason jars, let to cool for a couple of minutes and refrigerate for at least 4 hours.
7. Serve and enjoy!

Salmon Tortellini Soup

Preparation time: 5 minutes
Cook time: 15 minutes
Total time: 20 minutes
Yield: 4

Ingredients:
- 2/3 cup of diced onion
- 2 cloves garlic, minced
- 1-2 strips bacon, diced
- 12-16 oz. of frozen boneless salmon, cut into 3-4 pieces
- 1 (10 ounces) of package frozen mixed vegetables
- 10 oz. of frozen tortellini
- 1 quart chicken or vegetable broth
- 1 teaspoon of paprika
- 1 teaspoon of Old Bay seasoning, optional
- 2-3 handfuls fresh baby spinach

Cooking Instructions:
1. Press the Sauté function on your Instant Pot and add the chopped bacon.
2. Add the onions and garlic and cook for about 3 minutes, stirring constantly. Press the Cancel function.
3. Add the frozen salmon, frozen vegetables, frozen tortellini, broth and seasonings into the bottom of your Instant Pot and give everything a good stir.
4. Close and lock the lid in place and ensure that the valve is in sealing position. Select Manual, High Pressure for 6 minutes.
5. When the timer beeps, do a quick pressure release. Carefully open the lid and flake the salmon into chunks with a fork. Add in the fresh baby spinach.
6. Serve and enjoy!

Lemon Garlic Parmesan Shrimp Pasta

Preparation time: 20 minutes
Cook time: 3 minutes
Total time: 23 minutes
Servings: 8

Ingredients:
- 1 tablespoon of butter
- 6 garlic cloves, minced
- 3 ¾ cup of chicken broth
- 1 pound of thin spaghetti (whole wheat or white)
- 1 pound of raw deveined, peeled jumbo shrimp
- 1 teaspoon of kosher salt
- 1 teaspoon of black pepper
- 1 ½ cups of half and half or heavy cream, warmed
- 6 tablespoons of fresh lemon juice
- Zest from 1 lemon
- 2 cups of grated/shredded parmesan cheese
- 8 ounces fresh spinach

Cooking Instructions:
1. Press the Sauté function on your Instant Pot and add the butter to melt.
2. Add in the garlic cloves and cook for 30 seconds. Add the chicken broth and break up the spaghetti. Add the broken spaghetti and ensure that it is fully submerged in the broth.
3. Close and lock the lid in place and ensure that the valve is in sealing position. Select Manual, High Pressure for 3 minutes.
4. When the timer beeps, do a quick pressure release. Carefully open the lid and press the Sauté function. Add in the shrimp.
5. Add the salt, pepper, half and half, lemon juice, lemon zest, parmesan cheese and spinach. Give everything a good stir.
6. Sauté the contents until the shrimp are pink and spinach is wilted. It will take about 3 minutes if the shrimp are not frozen. Season with salt and pepper to taste.
7. Serve and enjoy!

Tomato Pasta with Tuna & Capers

Preparation time: 10 minutes
Cook time: 6 minutes
Total time: 16 minutes

Ingredients:
- 2 garlic cloves, sliced
- 2 tablespoons of olive oil
- 15 ounces can of fire-roasted diced tomatoes
- ½ of tomato tin or red wine
- 2 cups of pasta, (We used Orecchiette)
- Oregano, dried chilies, for seasoning
- Salt to taste
- Pepper to taste
- 3.5 ounces can of solid tuna in vegetable oil
- 2 tablespoons of capers
- Grated parmesan

Cooking Instructions:
1. Press the Sauté function on your Instant Pot and add the oil.
2. Add the garlic and cook until fragrant. Add the pasta, tomatoes and seasonings.
3. Add red wine into ½ of the empty tomato can and top with water. Add the cans into the bottom of your Instant Pot.
4. Close and lock the lid in place and ensure that the valve is in sealing position. Select Manual, High Pressure for 6 minutes.
5. When the timer beeps, do a quick pressure release. Carefully open the lid and add the tuna and capers. Give everything a good stir to combine.
6. Serve, topped with some freshly shaved parmesan and extra chilies.

Lemon Pepper Salmon

Preparation time: 5 minutes
Cook time: 10 minutes
Total time: 15 minutes
Servings: 3 -4

Ingredients:
- ¾ cup of water
- A few sprigs of parsley dill, tarragon, basil or a combo
- 1 lb. of salmon filet skin on
- 3 tsp. of ghee or other healthy fat divided
- ¼ tsp. of salt or to taste
- ½ tsp. of pepper or to taste
- ½ lemon, thinly sliced
- 1 zucchini, julienned
- 1 red bell pepper, julienned
- 1 carrot, julienned

Cooking Instructions:
1. Pour water and add the herbs into the bottom of your Instant Pot. Place the steamer rack and ensure that the handles are extended up.
2. Add the salmon, skin down on the steamer rack. Sprinkle the salmon with ghee/fat, season with salt and pepper on both sides, and cover with lemon slices.
3. Close and lock the lid in place and ensure that the valve is in sealing position. Select the Steam function and set to cook for 3 minutes.
4. When the timer beeps, do a quick pressure release. Press the "Warm/Cancel" function. Carefully open the lid and transfer the salmon to a bowl.
5. Remove herbs and discard. Add the veggies and secure the lid in place. Turn the Instant Pot on "Sauté" function and allow the veggies cook for about 2 minutes.
6. Add the remaining teaspoon of fat and pour a little of the sauce over them if desired. Give everything a good stir. Serve and enjoy!

Teriyaki Salmon

Preparation time: 10 minutes
Cook time: 8 minutes
Total time: 18 minutes
Serves: 2

Ingredients:
- 2 thick salmon fillets, 8 ounces each
- ½ cup of soy sauce
- ¼ cup of water
- ¼ cup of mirin
- 1 tbsp. of sesame oil
- 2 tsp. of sesame seeds
- 1 clove garlic, minced
- 1 tbsp. of freshly grated ginger
- 2 tbsp. of brown sugar
- 2-3 green onions, minced, for garnish

Cooking Instructions:
1. In a medium bowl, add together the soy sauce, water, mirin, sesame oil, sesame seeds, garlic, ginger and brown sugar.
2. Add the green onions and give everything a good whisk to combine. Add the salmon in two 6 inch square pans and pour half of the marinade over the salmon.
3. Place the salmon in the fridge and allow to marinate for about 30 minutes. Pour 1 cup of water into the bottom of your Instant Pot and place the trivet.
4. Add the prepared pans inside, stacking them to form an X shape. Close and lock the lid in place and ensure that the valve is in sealing position.
5. Select Manual, High Pressure for 8 minutes. Pour the remaining marinade into a small sauté pan over medium high heat on the stove top.
6. In a separate bowl, mix 1 tbsp. of cornstarch with 1 tbsp. of water and give everything a good whisk to combine. Gently pour in the cornstarch slurry when the marinade comes to a simmer.
7. Whisk everything until thickened, 1-2 minutes and reserve aside. When the timer beeps, do a quick pressure release.
8. Carefully open the lid and stir. Drizzle the teriyaki sauce over the dish and garnish with the set aside green onion.
9. Serve warm over rice and enjoy!

Tuna Noodle Casserole

Preparation time: 10 minutes
Cook time: 4 minutes
Total time: 14 minutes

Ingredients:
- 2 stalks celery, sliced
- 1-2 carrots, peeled & chopped, optional
- ¼ cup of diced onions, optional
- 1 cup of frozen Peas
- 1 ½ cups of hot water
- ¾ cup of milk
- 12 ounces of uncooked Wide Egg Noodles
- 2 cans of Tuna packed in water, drained
- 1 can Cream of Celery or Cream of Mushroom Soup
- 1-2 tablespoons of butter
- Salt to taste
- Pepper to taste
- Cheese, optional

Cooking Instructions:
1. Turn the Instant Pot on Sauté function and add the butter.
2. Once hot, add the celery, carrots, and onions. Cook the ingredients the onion has soften for about 2 to 3 minutes.
3. Add the water and milk. Cook until it comes to a soft boil stirring, frequently to avoid burning the milk.
4. When it's boiling, add in the noodles, cream soup, and tuna and give everything a good mix. Close and lock the lid in place.
5. Select Manual, High Pressure for 4 minutes. When the timer beeps, do a quick pressure release.
6. Carefully remove the lid and stir in the peas, season with salt and pepper to taste and cheese if desired.
7. Serve and enjoy!

Seafood Corn Chowder

Preparation time: 15 minutes
Cook time: 7 minutes
Total time: 22 minutes
Yield: 4

Ingredients:
- 1 lb. of shrimp, scallops, fish, crab
- 4 tbsp. of butter
- 1 cup of onion, chopped
- 3 cloves fresh garlic, minced
- 2 cups of corn kernels
- 2 cups of carrots, chopped into 1.5 inch chunks
- 8 oz. of cremini mushrooms, cut in half
- 2 cups of string beans, cut in half
- 1 lb. potatoes peeled and cubed
- 32 oz. of chicken stock/broth
- ¼ cup of dry sherry wine
- 1 fresh lemon
- ½ cup of heavy whipping cream

Seasonings:
- 2 ½ tsp. of ground celery seed
- 2 ½ tsp. of ground mustard seed
- ¼ + 1/8 tsp. of allspice
- 2 tsp. of dried parsley flakes
- 1/8 +1/16 tsp. of ground cardamom
- 1/8 +1/16 tsp. of ground cinnamon
- ¾ tsp. of paprika
- 3/8 tsp. of ground ginger
- ¼ tsp. of freshly ground black pepper
- 1 ½ tsp. of sea salt
- 1/8 tsp. of ground white pepper
- 1/8 tsp. of crushed red pepper flakes
- 2 whole bay leaves

Cooking Instructions:
1. Turn on the Instant Pot on Sauté function and add the butter to melt. Add the onions and garlic and cook for about 3 minutes, or until onions starts to brown.
2. Press the Cancel function. Add ½ cup of broth to pot and scrape any browned bits stuck to the bottom of the pot.
3. Add all vegetables and seasonings. Add the sherry and squeeze in ½ lemon. Add the remaining broth. Close and lock the lid in place.
4. Select Manual, High Pressure for 7 minutes. When the timer beeps, do a natural pressure release for about 15 minutes.

5. Carefully open the lid and add the shrimp or scallops and/or fish. Press the Sauté function, add the cream and stir in to hot broth until fully cooked for a couple of minutes.
6. Serve and enjoy!

Shrimp & Pasta

Ingredients:
- 2 pounds of shrimp
- 2 tablespoons of oil
- 2 tablespoons of butter
- 1 tablespoon of garlic, minced
- ½ cup of white wine
- ½ cup of chicken stock
- Pasta or cooked rice
- 1 tablespoon of lemon juice
- Parsley for garnish
- Salt to taste
- Pepper to taste

Cooking Instructions:
1. Press the Sauté function on your Instant Pot and add the butter to melt.
2. Once the butter has melted, add the garlic and sauté the garlic until fragrant. Add the white wine and chicken stock to scrape up any browned bits stuck to the bottom of the pot.
3. Press the Cancel function and add the shrimp. Close and lock the lid in place and ensure that the valve is in sealing position.
4. Select the Meat/Stew function and set to cook for 1 minute. When the timer beeps, do a natural pressure release for about 5 minutes.
5. Carefully open the lid and stir in the cooked pasta or rice. Add the lemon juice, salt and pepper to taste.
6. To cook rice in your instant pot, pour 2 cups of rice along with 3 cups of water into the bottom of your Instant Pot. Close and lock the lid in place.
7. Select the Rice function. When the timer beeps, do a natural pressure release for about 10 minutes.
8. To cook pasta in your instant pot, pour 2 cups of pasta to 3 cups of water into the bottom of your Instant Pot. Select the Soup function and set to cook for 8 minutes.
9. When the timer beeps, do a quick pressure release. Carefully remove the lid. Serve and enjoy!

10-Minute Instant Pot Salmon

Preparation time: 10 minutes
Cook time: 5 minutes
Total time: 15 minutes
Serves: 4
Ingredients:
- 3 medium lemon
- ¾ cup of water
- 4 fillet salmon
- 1 bunch dill weed, fresh
- 1 tbsp. of butter, unsalted
- ¼ tsp. of salt
- ¼ tsp. of black pepper, ground

Optional:
- 1 cup of brown rice, raw
- 4 cups of green beans

Cooking Instructions:
1. Add ¼ cup of fresh lemon juice and pour ¾ cup of water into the bottom of your Instant Pot.
2. Place the metal steamer insert and add the salmon fillets, frozen, on top of the steamer insert.
3. Sprinkle fresh dill on top of the salmon fillets and add 1 slice of fresh lemon on top of each one.
4. Close and lock the lid in place and ensure that the valve is in sealing position. Select Manual, High Pressure for 5 minutes.
5. When the cooking cycle has completed, do a quick pressure release. Carefully remove the lid and season with salt and pepper to taste.
6. Serve with butter, extra dill and lemon, and enjoy!

New England Clam Chowder

Preparation time: 10 minutes
Cook time: 5 minutes
Total time: 15 minutes

Ingredients:
- 3 pieces of bacon
- 1 onion, diced
- 1 stalk of celery, diced
- 2 cups of clam juice
- 3-4 potatoes, peeled and cubed
- 1 lb. of clam meat
- 1 cup of cream
- 2 cups of water

Spices:
- 1 bay leaf
- 1 tsp. of thyme
- 1 tsp. of salt
- 1 tsp. of pepper

Cooking Instructions:
1. Place the bacon into the bottom of your Instant Pot and press the Sauté function. Sauté the bacon until done.
2. Add the onion and celery. Sauté the contents for about 4 minutes or until they have softened. Add the clam juice, potatoes, and spice ingredients.
3. Add water, and give everything a good mix. Close and lock the lid in place and ensure that the valve is in sealing position.
4. Select Manual, High Pressure for 5 minutes. When the timer beeps, do a natural pressure release for about 10 minutes.
5. Carefully remove the lid and add in the clams. Sauté for additional 5 minutes to cook the clams. Add the cream and sauté until the soup is hot.
6. Serve and enjoy!

INSTANT POT POULTRY RECIPES

Hawaiian Shredded Chicken

Preparation time: 10 minutes
Cook time: 5 minutes
Total time: 15 minutes
Servings: 5

Ingredients:
- 1 jar barbecue sauce 20 ounces
- 1 cup of chunk pineapple
- 3 - 4 chicken breasts or 2 large ones cut in half, boneless / skinless
- 1 bag of flour tortillas pkg. small
- ¾ cup of water
- Avocado sliced, optional
- 1 cup of pineapple juice
- 1 onion, sliced
- 1 tablespoon of soy sauce, optional
- 1 cup of cheese

Cooking Instructions:
1. Add ½ jar of barbecue sauce into the bottom of your Instant Pot and place the chicken breasts on top.
2. Squeeze the remaining half of jar on top of the chicken. Add the ¾ cup of water into the pot. Add the chunks of pineapple, sliced onion and soy sauce if desired.
3. Give everything a good stir to coat the chicken. Close and lock the lid in place and ensure that the valve is in sealing position.
4. Select the Poultry function and set to cook for 15 minutes. When the timer beeps, do a quick pressure release.
5. Carefully remove the lid and shred the chicken with two forks. Add small tortillas to make soft tacos with some cheese and avocado.
6. Serve on top of rice and enjoy!

Salsa Lime Chicken

Preparation time: 5 minutes
Cook time: 25 minutes
Total time: 30 minutes
Servings: 6

Ingredients:
- 3 chicken breasts
- 16 oz. of salsa
- Juice from 1 lime

Cooking Instructions:
1. Add the chicken breasts into the bottom of your Instant Pot.
2. Pour salsa over the chicken. Add the lime juice on top of the salsa.
3. Close and lock the lid in place and ensure that the valve is in sealing position.
4. Select the Poultry function and adjust to cook for 25 minutes.
5. When the timer beeps, do a quick pressure release.
6. Carefully remove the lid and give everything a good stir.
7. Serve and enjoy!

Chicken Quinoa Casserole

Preparation time: 15 minutes
Cook time: 20 minutes
Total time: 35 minutes
Servings: 6

Ingredients:
- 6 chicken thighs boneless, skinless, cubed
- ½ onion, sliced
- 3 stalks celery, sliced
- 1.5 cup of green beans fresh, ends cut off, cut in half
- 1/3 cabbage, cut into chunks
- 4 tablespoons of pesto
- ½ teaspoon of salt
- ¼ teaspoon of chili powder
- ¼ teaspoon of paprika
- ½ teaspoon of garlic salt
- ¼ teaspoon of pepper
- ½ teaspoon of oregano
- ¾ teaspoon of garlic minced, We used jarred
- 2-2.5 cup of chicken broth
- 1 cup of quinoa not quick quinoa, traditional

Cooking Instructions:
1. Add the cubed chicken thighs into the bottom of your Instant Pot and add the onion.
2. Add celery, green beans and all the spices. Give everything a good stir until combined. Add the cabbage cut into chunks on top of everything.
3. Pour the chicken broth. Pour 1 ¾ cup of broth if you are making chicken quinoa casserole. Add 2-2.5 cups of broth if you're making chicken cabbage soup.
4. Select Poultry function and set to cook for 13 minutes. When the timer beeps, do a quick pressure release.
5. Carefully remove the lid and add 1 cup of uncooked traditional quinoa. Give everything a good stir.
6. Close and lock the lid in place and ensure that the valve is in sealing position. Select Manual, High Pressure for 4 minutes.
7. When the timer beeps, do a quick pressure release. Carefully remove the lid and give everything a good stir.
8. Serve and enjoy!

Honey Garlic Chicken

Preparation time: 5 minutes
Cook time: 20 minutes
Total time: 25 minutes
Servings: 4

Ingredients:
- 1/3 cup of honey
- 4 cloves garlic, minced
- ½ cup of low sodium soy sauce
- ½ cup of no salt ketchup
- ½ tsp. of dried oregano
- 2 tbsp. of chopped fresh parsley
- 1 tbsp. of sesame seed oil
- 4 - 6 bone-in, skinless chicken thighs
- Salt to taste
- Fresh ground pepper, to taste
- ½ tbsp. of toasted sesame seeds, for garnish
- Sliced green onions, for garnish

Cooking Instructions:
1. In a medium bowl, combine together the honey, minced garlic, soy sauce, ketchup, oregano and parsley.
2. Give everything a good mix until well combined and set aside. Press the Sauté function on your Instant Pot and add the sesame oil.
3. Generously season the chicken thighs with salt and pepper. Place the chicken thighs into the bottom of your Instant Pot.
4. Cook for about 2 to 3 minutes on each side. Add the prepared honey garlic sauce to the pot. Close and lock the lid in place.
5. Select the Poultry function and set to cook for 20 minutes. When the timer beeps, do a quick pressure release. Press the Cancel function.
6. Carefully remove the lid and transfer the chicken to a serving bowl. Add the sauce over the chicken. Garnish with toasted sesame seeds and green onions.
7. Serve and enjoy!

Creamy Italian Chicken Breasts

Preparation time: 10 minutes
Cook time: 8 minutes
Total time: 18 minutes
Servings: 4

Ingredients:
- 4 boneless skinless chicken breasts
- 1 cup of low sodium chicken broth
- 1 tsp. of minced garlic
- 1 tsp. of Italian seasoning
- ¼ tsp. of salt
- ¼ tsp. of black pepper
- 1/3 cup of heavy cream
- 1/3 cup of roasted red peppers
- 1 ½ tbsp. of corn starch
- 1 tbsp. of basil pesto

Cooking Instructions:
1. Add the chicken breasts into the bottom of your Instant Pot and pour the broth. Sprinkle with garlic, Italian seasoning, salt and pepper.
2. Close and lock the lid in place and ensure that the valve is in sealing position. Select Manual, High Pressure for 8 minutes.
3. When the timer beeps, do a natural pressure release for about 5 minutes, then quick release any remaining pressure.
4. Carefully remove the lid and transfer the chicken breasts on a cutting board. Press the Sauté function and stir in the cream, red peppers, corn starch and pesto.
5. Give everything a good mix and cook for about 3-4 minutes, until thickened. Return the chicken back into the pot.
6. Serve with the sauce over top and enjoy!

Chicken Marsala

Preparation time: 5 minutes
Cook time: 15 minutes
Total time: 20 minutes
Serves: 4

Ingredients:
- 2 tablespoons of butter
- Flour
- 1 - 1.5 lb. of thinly sliced chicken breasts
- 8-12 oz. of sliced mushrooms (We used baby portobellas)
- 4 oz. of pancetta, finely cubed
- 2/3 cup of marsala cooking wine
- 1 cup of chicken broth
- 2 cloves garlic, minced
- 1 tablespoon of cornstarch + 1 tablespoon of water
- Fresh parsley to garnish

Cooking Instructions:
1. Press the Sauté function on your Instant Pot and add the butter to melt. Add the chicken breasts in flour on both sides.
2. Add the dredged chicken breasts into the bottom of your Instant Pot and allow them to brown in the butter for 1-2 minutes on each side.
3. Transfer the chicken breasts to a bowl and set aside. Add the garlic, pancetta, mushrooms and Marsala wine and cook for about 2 minutes.
4. Press the Cancel function. Add the chicken breasts into the pot along with chicken broth, nestling chicken down into the mushrooms.
5. Select Manual, High Pressure for 8 minutes. When the timer beeps, do a quick pressure release. Carefully open the lid and transfer the chicken breasts to a bowl.
6. Press the Sauté function and allow to bubble for about 1 minute. In a medium bowl, mix together the cornstarch and water.
7. Pour the mixture into the pot and allow to simmer for about 5-10 minutes, stirring occasionally while sauce thickens.
8. Add the chicken on serving bowl, spoon mushroom sauce over chicken, garnish with parsley.
9. Serve hot and enjoy!

White Chicken Chili

Preparation time: 10 minutes
Cook time: 5 minutes
Total time: 15 minutes
Servings: 6

Ingredients:
- 1 chicken breast cubed, about 2 cups
- 3 tablespoons of olive oil
- 1 tablespoon of minced garlic
- 14-16 ounces of chicken broth
- 1 small can of diced chilies
- 1 cup of canned corn, drained
- 1 jar salsa Verde 16 ounces
- 2 cans of white beans
- 1 tablespoon of cornstarch
- Salt to taste
- Toppings: sour cream, avocado, spicy jack cheese shredded
- ½ onion, diced

Cooking Instructions:
1. Press the Sauté function on your Instant Pot and add the olive oil. Add the garlic, and onions and sauté until onions are softened.
2. Add the cubed chicken and sauté for additional 3 minutes. Press the Cancel function. Add the salsa Verde, broth, chilies, white beans, corn and a pinch of salt.
3. Close and lock the lid in place and ensure that the valve is in sealing position. Select Manual, High Pressure for 5 minutes.
4. When the timer beeps, do a quick pressure release. Carefully remove the lid. In a medium bowl, ladle some of the chili liquid with cornstarch and stir.
5. Add the mixture into the pot and give everything a good stir to thicken. Ladle into your serving bowl and top with spicy jack cheese, avocado and sour cream!
6. Serve immediately and enjoy!

Chicken Cordon Bleu

Preparation time: 12 minutes
Cook time: 15 minutes
Total time: 27 minutes
Servings: 4

Ingredients:
- 2 cups of panko breadcrumbs
- 1 teaspoon of salt
- ½ teaspoon of pepper
- 3-4 chicken breast halves boneless, skinless
- 8 slices deli ham, thinly sliced
- 4 slices Swiss cheese
- ½ cup of butter, melted
- 1 cup of chicken broth

Cooking Instructions:
1. Combine together the Panko, salt, and pepper in a medium bowl and set aside. Pound the chicken breast to 1/2" thickness.
2. Add 2 slices of ham over each chicken breast and add a slice of Swiss cheese over the ham. Then, roll chicken up tightly.
3. Dip each of the chicken roll in the melted butter, then roll in breadcrumbs. Add the chicken breast into the bottom of your Instant Pot.
4. Pour the rest of the melted butter over the chicken and place the chicken broth in the cracks between the chicken breasts.
5. Close and lock the lid in place and ensure that the valve is in sealing position. Select Manual, High Pressure for 8 minutes.
6. When the timer beeps, do a natural pressure release for about 5 minutes, then quick release any remaining pressure.
7. Carefully open the lid and transfer the chicken to a serving bowl. Serve immediately and enjoy!

Orange Chicken

Preparation time: 10 minutes
Cook time: 4 minutes
Total time: 14 minutes
Servings: 4

Ingredients:
- 2 chicken breasts boneless skinless, cubed
- 2 cups of barbecue sauce
- 3 tablespoons of soy sauce
- 1 tablespoon of cornstarch
- ¼ cup of orange marmalade
- ¼ onion, cut into large pieces - optional
- Chives or green onion to garnish
- ¼ cup of water

Cooking Instructions:
1. Add the cubed chicken breasts into the bottom of your Instant Pot and add the barbecue sauce, water, onion, and soy sauce.
2. Give everything a good stir to coat the chicken pieces. Close and lock the lid in place and ensure that the valve is in sealing position.
3. Select Manual, High Pressure for 4 minutes. When the timer beeps, do a quick pressure release. Carefully remove the lid and transfer the chicken pieces to a plate.
4. Press the Sauté function. In a medium bowl, mix together the cornstarch and add some hot barbeque sauce from pot.
5. Give the mixture a good whisk and pour back into the pot. Add marmalade and give everything a good stir.
6. Let the contents to bubble for about 2 minutes. Add the chicken pieces and stir.
7. Serve over rice and enjoy!

Pineapple Chicken Breasts

Preparation time: 10 minutes
Cook time: 10 minutes
Total time: 30 minutes
Servings: 4

Ingredients:
- 4 boneless skinless chicken breasts
- 1 398ml can pineapple chunks with juice 14 ounces
- 3 tbsp. of sodium-reduced soy sauce
- 3 tbsp. of brown sugar packed
- ½ tsp. of salt
- Pinch of black pepper
- 1 tbsp. of corn starch
- 1 tbsp. of water

Cooking Instructions:
1. Add the pineapple chunks with juice, soy sauce, sugar, salt and pepper into the bottom of your Instant Pot.
2. Give everything a good stir to combine. Place the chicken breasts on top of the pineapple. Close and lock the lid in place and ensure that the valve is in sealing position.
3. Select Manual, High Pressure for 10 minutes. When the timer beeps, do a quick pressure release for about 10 minutes, then quick release any remaining pressure.
4. Carefully open the lid and stir. Press the Sauté function. In a medium bowl, mix together the corn starch and water. Add the mixture into the sauce and stir.
5. Cook and stir frequently until the sauce has thickened. Press the Cancel function.
6. Serve over rice, noodles or with a side of veggies.

BBQ Chicken with Potatoes

Preparation time: 10 minutes
Cook time: 15 minutes
Total time: 25 minutes

Ingredients:
- 2 lbs. of frozen chicken
- 1 cup of favorite BBQ sauce
- ½ cup of water
- 1 tbsp. of Italian seasoning
- 1 tbsp. of minced garlic
- 2-3 large potatoes, chopped
- 1 red onion, sliced

Cooking Instructions:
1. Add all the ingredients into the bottom of your Instant Pot.
2. Close and lock the lid in place and ensure that the valve is in sealing position. Select the Poultry function and adjust to cook for 15 minutes.
3. When the timer beeps, do a natural pressure release for about 10 minutes. Carefully remove the lid and transfer the chicken to a bowl.
4. Shred the chicken with two forks. Add the chicken back into the pot and give everything a good stir to coat.
5. Serve and enjoy!

Spicy Honey Chicken

Preparation time: 15 minutes
Cook time: 4 minutes
Total time 19 minutes
Servings: 6

Ingredients:
- 4 chicken breasts, cut into bite size chunks
- 1 tablespoon of brown sugar
- 1 tablespoon of minced ginger
- 1.5 tablespoon of minced garlic
- 3 tablespoons of honey
- ¼ cup of soy sauce
- 1 tablespoon of Sriracha
- 1 teaspoon of Worcestershire Sauce
- ½ onion, diced
- 1 tablespoon of sesame seeds, optional
- 2 green onions, optional
- 2 tablespoons of cornstarch

Cooking Instructions:
1. Add the chicken and onions into the bottom of your Instant Pot.
2. In a medium bowl, mix together all of the remaining ingredients (except the cornstarch) with a fork.
3. Pour the mixture over the chicken. Close and lock the lid in place and ensure that the valve is in sealing position.
4. Select Manual, High Pressure for 4 minutes. When the timer beeps, do a quick pressure release. Carefully remove the lid.
5. In a medium bowl, ladle some of the hot sauce, add the corn starch and whisk. Press the Sauté function, normal and let to bubble for a couple of minutes to thicken.
6. Serve over rice and enjoy!

Chicken Parmesan Casserole

Preparation time: 10 minutes
Cook time: 10 minutes
Total time: 20 minutes
Servings: 5

Ingredients:
- 2 chicken breasts, cut into chunks
- ½ onion, diced
- 2 tablespoons of olive oil
- 1 teaspoon of salt
- 1 teaspoon of basil
- 1 jar spaghetti sauce 24 ounces
- 2 cups of water
- 2 cups of noodles, uncooked, (We used rotini)
- 1 teaspoon of garlic, minced
- 2 tablespoons of butter
- 1/3 cup of bread crumbs
- 1 cup of parmesan cheese

Cooking Instructions:
1. Turn on the Instant Pot on Sauté, normal function and add the olive oil.
2. Add the chicken pieces and sauté for about 1-2 minutes. Add the diced onions and garlic, sauté for additional 3 minutes.
3. Add the salt, basil, spaghetti sauce, water, and give everything a good stir. Add the 2 cups of uncooked noodles.
4. Push down to noodles to completely submerge in the liquid and do not stir. Close and lock the lid in place and ensure that the valve is in sealing position.
5. Select Manual, High Pressure for 10 minutes. When the timer beeps, do a quick pressure release. Carefully remove the lid and stir in 2/3 cup of grated parmesan.
6. In a medium bowl, dissolve the butter and stir in 1/3 cup of bread crumbs and 1/3 cup of grated parmesan.
7. Ladle into a serving bowl and sprinkle bread crumb mixture on top.
8. Serve and enjoy!

INSTANT POT BEAN & RICE RECIPES

Coconut Rice Pudding

Preparation time: 10 minutes
Cook time: 14 minutes
Total time: 24 minutes

Ingredients:
- 1 cup of uncooked rice
- ½ cup of sugar
- 1 cup of water
- 1.5 tablespoon of butter
- 1 can coconut milk (13.5 ounces)
- ¼ cup of milk
- 1 egg
- ¼ cup of evaporated milk
- ½ cup of shredded sweetened coconut

Cooking Instructions:
1. Press the Sauté function on your Instant Pot and add the butter to melt.
2. Add the rice and give everything a good stir to coat. Add the coconut milk, regular milk, ¼ cup of coconut, and sugar and give everything a good stir.
3. Close and lock the lid in place and ensure that the valve is in sealing position. Select Manual, High Pressure for 14 minutes. When the timer beeps, do a quick pressure release.
4. Carefully remove the lid. Press the Cancel function. In a medium bowl, whisk together the evaporated milk and egg. Allow the rice pudding to bubble before adding half milk/egg mixture and give everything a good stir to combine.
5. Add rest of the ¼ cup of coconut, and the remaining milk/egg mixture. Let the contents to bubble again, stir gently to combine.
6. Press the Cancel function and ladle the coconut rice pudding into serving plates. Serve immediately and enjoy!

Refried Beans

Preparation time: 10 minutes
Cook time: 40 minutes
Total time: 50 minutes

Ingredients:
- 1 cup of pinto beans, sorted and rinsed
- 2 cloves garlic, chopped
- 1 onion, chopped
- 1 jalapeño, minced
- 1 bay leaf
- 1 tbsp. of sea salt
- 3 cups of filtered water
- ¼ cup of avocado oil

Cooking Instructions:
1. Place the beans, water, bay leaf and garlic into the bottom of your Instant Pot.
2. Close and lock the lid in place and ensure that the valve is in sealing position. Select Manual, High Pressure for 40 minutes.
3. When the timer beeps, do a natural pressure release for about 10 minutes. Carefully remove the lid and transfer the beans and water to a large bowl.
4. Press the Sauté function and olive oil. Add the onion, jalapeño, and add the sea salt. Add the beans and water back into the Instant Pot.
5. Continue to cook on Sauté function. Mash the beans with the back of your slotted spoon and stir the beans.
6. Cook for a couple of minutes, until the refried beans are thickened.
7. Serve and enjoy!

American Spanish Rice

Preparation time: 10 minutes
Cook time: 12 minutes
Total time: 22 minutes

Ingredients:
- 1 jar spaghetti sauce, 28 ounces
- 1 onion, chopped
- 3 peppers, chopped
- 1 lb. of ground turkey or beef
- 1 tablespoon of chili powder
- 2 cups of rice
- 2 cups of water
- Cheddar cheese, optional

Cooking Instructions:
1. Press the Sauté function on your Instant Pot and add the onions. Add the peppers.
2. Add the ground turkey into the bottom of your Instant Pot and sauté the meat. Add the jar of sauce and pour in 2 cups of water.
3. Give everything a good stir and add the 2 cups of rice. Close and lock the lid in place and ensure that the valve is in sealing position.
4. Select Manual, High Pressure for 12 minutes. When the timer beeps, do a quick pressure release.
5. Carefully remove the lid and ladle into a serving bowl. Garnish with cheddar cheese and green onions if desired.
6. Serve and enjoy!

Cinnamon Brown Rice Pudding

Preparation time: 5 minutes
Cook time: 35 minutes
Total time: 40 minutes
Servings: 4

Ingredients:
- 1 cup of short grain brown rice
- 1 ½ cups of water
- 1 tablespoon of vanilla extract
- 1 cinnamon stick
- 1 tablespoon of butter
- 1 cup of raisins
- 3 tablespoons of honey
- ½ cup of heavy cream

Cooking Instructions:
1. Place the rice, water, vanilla, cinnamon stick, and butter into the bottom of your Instant Pot.
2. Close and lock the lid in place and ensure that the valve is in sealing position. Select Manual, High Pressure for 20 minutes.
3. When the timer beeps, do a natural pressure release for about 10 minutes. Carefully remove the lid and discard cinnamon stick.
4. Stir in raisins, honey and cream. Select the Sauté function and adjust less. Sauté for about 5 minutes.
5. Serve hot and enjoy!

Mexican Beef Rice

Preparation time: 9 minutes
Cook time 16: minutes
Total time: 25 minutes
Servings: 4 - 6

Ingredients:
- 1 tbsp. of olive oil
- 1 lb. of lean ground beef
- 1 cup of diced red onion
- 1 tsp. of chili powder Hatch chili powder is okay
- ½ tsp. of ground cumin
- ½ tsp. of salt
- 1 cup of long grain white rice, rinsed and drained
- 2 cups of water
- 2 cups of chunky salsa
- 15 oz. of black beans, rinsed and drained
- 1 cup of cooked corn kernels
- 2 tbsp. of chopped fresh cilantro
- 1 cup of shredded cheese Cheddar, Monterey Jack and Cheddar, or 4 Cheese Mexican blend
- Boston lettuce, optional

Cooking Instructions:
1. Press the Sauté function on your Instant Pot and add the ground beef.
2. Add the onion, chili powder, cumin, and salt. Sauté, stirring and breaking up beef for about 5 minutes or until beef has browned.
3. Add the rice, water, and salsa. Give everything a good stir to combine. Close and lock lid the lid in place and ensure that the valve is in sealing position.
4. Select Manual, High Pressure for 8 minutes. When the timer beeps, do a quick pressure release.
5. Press the Sauté function. Carefully remove the lid and add the black beans, corn, and cilantro.
6. Give everything a good stir to combine. Sauté, stirring for about 3 minutes or until the beans and corn are heated through.
7. Ladle the beans to a serving bowl and top with cheese. Serve with Boston lettuce leaves to make lettuce wraps and enjoy!

13 Bean Soup

Ingredients:
- 1.5 cups of 16 bean soup mix various beans, lentils, peas
- 1 ham bone
- 1 medium onion, chopped
- 1 diced tomato
- 1 cup of carrots, diced
- 2/3 cup of celery, diced
- 2 tsp. of chili powder
- 1 tsp. of garlic powder
- 1 tsp. of sea salt
- ¼ tsp. of black pepper

Cooking Instructions:
1. Add the beans along with 3 cups of water into the bottom of your Instant Pot.
2. Close and lock the lid in place and ensure that the valve is in sealing position. Select Manual, High Pressure for 10 minutes.
3. When the timer beeps, do a natural pressure release for about 10 minutes. Carefully remove the lid and rinse and drain the beans.
4. Add the beans back into the Instant Pot with the ham bone. Close and lock the lid in place. Select the Bean function.
5. When the timer beeps, do a natural pressure release for about 10 minutes. Carefully open the lid and remove the ham bone.
6. Add the remaining ingredients. Select the Soup function and cook for 20 minutes. When the timer beeps, do a natural pressure release.
7. Serve and enjoy!

Millet & Pinto Bean Chili

Preparation time: 3 hours
Cook time: 40 minutes
Total time: 3 hours 40 minutes
Yield: 6

Ingredients:
- 1 tablespoon of olive oil
- ½ onion, chopped
- 2 garlic cloves, minced
- 1 bell pepper, chopped
- 2 tablespoon of chili powder
- 2 teaspoons of cocoa or cacao powder
- 1 teaspoon of paprika
- 1 teaspoon of garlic powder
- ½ teaspoon of ground cinnamon
- ½ teaspoon of red chili flakes
- 1 bay leaf
- 2 cups pinto beans (soaked for at least 3 hours)
- 1 cup of millet (uncooked)
- 1 cup of sweet corn kernels (fresh or frozen)
- ¼ cup of chopped fresh cilantro
- ¼ cup of chopped fresh parsley
- 2 cups of fire roasted diced tomatoes
- 7 cups of vegetable stock or water
- 1 tablespoon of coconut sugar
- 1 teaspoon of apple cider vinegar
- 1 cup of fresh mixed greens
- Sea salt to taste
- Fresh cilantro or parsley, for garnish

Cooking Instructions:
1. Press the Sauté function on your Instant Pot and add the oil. Add the garlic and bell peppers.
2. Cook, stirring frequently for about 5 minutes. Add the spices - chili powder through bay leaf. Cook for additional 1 minute.
3. Add the pinto beans, millet, corn, cilantro and parsley. Cook, stirring constantly on Sauté function for additional 1 minute.
4. Press the Cancel function. Add in tomatoes and vegetable stock. Close and lock the lid in place and ensure that the valve is in sealing position.
5. Select Manual, High Pressure for 33 minutes. When the timer beeps, do a quick pressure release. Carefully remove the lid and stir in sugar, vinegar, greens.
6. Season with salt to taste. Serve immediately garnish with cilantro and/or parsley if desired.
7. Serve and enjoy!

Rice Pudding

Preparation time: 10 minutes
Cook time: 20 minutes
Total time: 30 minutes
Servings: 6

Ingredients:
- 2 cups of raw whole milk or dairy-free milk of choice
- 1 ¼ cups of water
- 1 cup of basmati rice
- ¾ cup of heavy cream OR coconut cream
- ¼ cup of maple syrup
- 1/8 tsp. of sea salt
- 1 vanilla bean OR 1 tsp. of vanilla extract

Cooking Instructions:
1. Add the rice in fine mesh colander and rinse in cleaning running water. Add the rice into the bottom of your Instant Pot.
2. Add the water, milk, maple syrup, and sea salt and give everything a good stir. Close and lock the lid in place and ensure that the valve is in sealing position.
3. Select the Porridge function and adjust to cook for 20 minutes. When the timer beeps, do a natural pressure release for about 10 minutes.
4. Carefully remove the lid and add the cream and vanilla. Give everything a good stir until well mixed.
5. Serve with optional toppings and enjoy!

Yellow Rice with Peas & Corn

Preparation time: 5 minutes
Cook time: 15 minutes
Total time: 20 minutes
Serves: 6

Ingredients:
- 2 cups of basmati rice, rinsed 4 times in cold water
- 3 tbsp. of olive oil
- 1 onion, diced small
- ¼ tsp. of salt
- 3 tbsp. of chopped cilantro stalks (optional)
- 2 large cloves of garlic, finely diced
- 1 heaped tsp. of turmeric powder
- 1 cup of frozen sweet corn kernels
- 1 cup of frozen garden peas
- 2¼ cups of chicken stock
- A dollop of butter, to finish (optional, olive oil)

Cooking Instructions:
1. Press the Sauté function on your Instant Pot and add the olive oil. Add the onions and salt and sauté for about 5 minutes, stirring occasionally until softened.
2. Add the chopped cilantro, garlic and turmeric powder and give everything a good stir. Add the corn, peas and rice and pour over the chicken stock.
3. Give everything a good stir and press the Keep Warm/Cancel function. Close and lock the lid and ensure that the valve is in sealing position.
4. Place and lock the lid, make sure the steam releasing handle is pointing to Sealing. Select Manual, High Pressure for 4 minutes.
5. When the timer beeps, do a natural pressure release for about 5 minutes, then quick release any remaining pressure.
6. Carefully remove the lid and add a dollop of butter, if desired. Allow the butter to melt into the rice, then fluff it with a fork. Transfer to a bowl.
7. Serve and enjoy!

Red Beans and Rice

Servings: 6
Preparation time: 20 minutes
Cook time: 45 minutes
Total time: 1 hour 5 minutes

Ingredients:
- 1 ½ cups of white long grain rice
- 1 tbsp. of olive oil
- 1 (12.8-oz.) package smoked andouille sausage, thinly sliced
- 4 cloves garlic, minced
- 1 onion, diced
- 1 green bell pepper, diced
- 2 stalks celery, thinly sliced
- 1 lb. of dry red beans
- 1 ½ tsp. of Cajun seasoning
- 1 tsp. of dried oregano
- ½ tsp. of dried basil
- ¼ tsp. of dried sage
- 2 sprigs fresh thyme
- 2 bay leaves
- 4 cup of low sodium vegetable broth
- Kosher salt
- Freshly ground black pepper, to taste
- 1 tsp. of hot sauce, or more, to taste
- 2 green onions, thinly sliced

Cooking Instructions:
1. Add the rice in a large saucepan along with 3 cups of water and cook according to package instructions; set aside.
2. Press the Sauté function on your Instant Pot and add the olive oil. Add the sausage and cook for about 4 minutes, stirring frequently, until sausage is lightly browned.
3. Place the sausage to a paper towel-lined plate and reserve aside. Add the garlic, onion, bell pepper and celery.
4. Sauté, stirring occasionally, until tender for about 2-3 minutes. Add in sausage, red beans, Cajun seasoning, oregano, basil, sage and thyme into the bottom of your Instant Pot.
5. Add the bay leaves and vegetable broth; season with salt and pepper, to taste. Close and lock the lid in place and ensure that the valve is in sealing position.
6. Select Manual, High Pressure for 30-35 minutes. When the timer beeps, do a natural pressure release for about 20 minutes. Carefully remove the lid.
7. Serve with rice and hot sauce, garnished with green onions, if desired.

Baked Beans

Preparation time: 10 minutes
Cook time: 5 hours 11 minutes
Total time: 5 hours 21 minutes

Ingredients:
- 1 lb. of small white beans
- 1 medium onion, minced
- 2 cloves garlic, minced
- ½ cup of molasses
- ½ cup of maple syrup
- 1 tbsp. of mustard powder
- 1/8 cup of balsamic vinegar
- ¼ tsp. of ground black pepper
- 4 cups of water or more to cover the beans
- 1 tsp. of sea salt

Cooking Instructions:
1. Add the beans and 3 cups of water into the bottom of your Instant Pot.
2. Close and lock the lid in place and ensure that the valve is in sealing position. Select Manual, High Pressure for 10 minutes.
3. When the timer beeps, do a natural pressure release for about 10 minutes. Carefully remove the lid and drain and rinse the beans.
4. Add the beans back into the bottom of your Instant Pot and add enough water to cover the beans. Add the remaining ingredients.
5. Close and lock the lid in place and ensure that the valve is in sealing position. Select the Bean function and adjust to cook for 45 minutes.
6. When the timer beeps, do a natural pressure release for about 10 minutes. Carefully remove the lid and give everything a good stir.
7. Serve and enjoy!

Rice Pilaf

Preparation time: 10 minutes
Cook time: 15 minutes
Total time: 25 minutes
Servings: 4

Ingredients:
- 2 180-mL rice cups (360 mL total) raw short grain white rice, rinsed 2 to 3 times in tap water
- 2 and ½ 180-ml rice cups chicken stock, or water
- 1 tbsp. of rice wine (or Japanese sake)
- 1 tbsp. of vegetable oil
- 1 cup of leftover meat, chopped
- 2 waxy potatoes, cubed
- 2 carrots, chopped
- 1 lb. of white mushrooms, halved
- 1 lb. of green beans, chopped
- 2 - 3 cups of kale with stem, chopped
- 2 tbsp. of soy sauce
- 1 tbsp. of oyster sauce
- Green onion, chopped for for garnish (Optional)
- Sriracha (Optional)

Cooking Instructions:
1. Add the rinsed white rice to a strainer and drain any remaining water. Meanwhile, prepare and chop all your vegetables and set aside.
2. Add together the rice, chicken stock, rice wine, and vegetable into the bottom of your Instant Pot.
3. Top the content in your pot with leftover meat, potato, carrot, mushrooms, green beans, and kale.
4. Add the soy sauce on top and avoid stirring. Close and lock the lid in place and ensure that the valve is in sealing position.
5. Select Manual, High Pressure for 8 minutes. When the timer beeps, do a quick pressure release.
6. Carefully open the lid and stir everything with a spatula. Add the oyster sauce and green onion and give everything a good mix.
7. Season with more sauce, if desired.
8. Serve immediately and enjoy!

INSTANT POT LAMB, BEEF & PORK RECIPES

Red Wine Beef Stew

Preparation time: 30 minutes
Cook time: 1 hour
Total time: 1 hour 30 minutes
Servings: 6

Ingredients:
- 3 tbsp. of olive oil
- 3 lbs. of boneless beef chuck cut into 1 1/2 inch pieces
- 2 cups of pearl onions frozen, thawed
- 1 ½ cups of red wine a big red, like a Syrah
- 1 lb. of carrots cut into 2-inch sections
- 6 dried figs stemmed
- 6 inch rosemary sprig
- 4 inch thyme sprig
- ½ tsp. of sale
- ½ tsp. of black pepper
- 1 tsp. of corn starch

Cooking Instructions:
1. Press the Sauté function on your Instant Pot and add the oil.
2. Add the beef and sauté, stirring occasionally for about 10 minutes and place the beef in a bowl.
3. Add the onions and sauté for about 5 minutes. Pour in the wine and deglaze the pot to remove any browned bits stuck to the bottom of the pot.
4. Add the carrots, figs, rosemary, thyme, salt and pepper. Return the beef back into the pot along with the accumulated juices in the bowl.
5. Close and lock the lid in place and ensure that the valve is in sealing position. Select Manual, High Pressure for 30 minutes.
6. When the timer beeps, do a natural pressure release for about 15 minutes, then quick release any remaining pressure.
7. Carefully open the lid and remove the thyme and rosemary. In a medium bowl, whisk together the cornstarch and 2 tsp. of water.
8. Pour the mixture into the pot and give everything a good stir until thickened about 1 minute.
9. Serve immediately over rice, noodles, steamed potatoes, or polenta if desired.

Asian Pork

Preparation time: 5 minutes
Cook time: 5 minutes
Total time: 10 minutes
Servings: 6

Ingredients:
- 2 pounds of pork loin, cut into about 2 inch chunks
- 1 teaspoon of sesame oil
- 1 cup of reduced sodium chicken or beef stock
- ½ cup of reduced sodium soy sauce
- 1/3 cup of balsamic vinegar
- ½ teaspoon of red pepper flakes
- 1 tablespoon of agave or honey
- 3 cloves garlic, minced
- 1 inch wedge fresh ginger, minced
- 8 oz. of mushrooms, chopped
- 1 tablespoon of cornstarch
- 2 tablespoons of water
- 3 stalks green onions, chopped
- Sesame seeds, for garnish
- Lettuce wraps/bib/romaine lettuce, tortilla wraps, salad, rice, optional for serving

Cooking Instructions:
1. Add the pork into the bottom of your Instant Pot and add the sesame oil.
2. Add the soy sauce, stock, balsamic vinegar, and red pepper flakes. Add the agave/honey, garlic, ginger, and mushrooms to the pot.
3. Give everything a good mix. Close and lock the lid in place. Select Manual, High Pressure for 20 minutes.
4. When the timer beeps, do a natural pressure release for about 11 minutes, then quick release any remaining pressure.
5. Carefully remove the lid and remove the pork to a bowl. Shred the pork and set aside. Press the Sauté function.
6. In a medium bowl, mix together the water and corn starch. Bring the pot to a boil and add the pour in the cornstarch mixture.
7. Give everything a good stir and cook for about 2 minutes or until the sauce has thickened.
8. Return the pork back into the pot and give everything a good stir to coat.
9. Serve immediately and enjoy!

Italian Beef

Preparation time: 10 minutes
Cook time: 90 minutes
Total time: 100 minutes

Ingredients:
- 2 tablespoons of olive oil extra virgin
- 1 2.5-3.5 pound of beef roast
- 12-16 ounces of sliced pepperoncini or banana peppers plus half the liquid
- 6 cloves garlic
- 2 cups of beef broth
- 1 tablespoon of Italian seasoning
- 1 teaspoon of onion powder

Cooking Instructions:
1. Press the Sauté function in your Instant Pot and add the roast.
2. Sauté the roast on all sides for about 4 minutes on each side. Press the Cancel function.
3. Close and lock the lid in place and ensure that the valve is in sealing position. Select the Meat / Stew function and adjust to cook for 90 minutes.
4. When the timer beeps, do a natural pressure release for about 15 minutes. Carefully unlock the lid and transfer the beef to a bowl.
5. Shred the beef with 2 forks. Return the beef back into the bottom of your Instant Pot and give everything a good stir.
6. Serve and enjoy!

Smoky Pork and Hominy Soup

Preparation time: 10 minutes
Cook time: 40 minutes
Total time: 50 minutes
Serves: 7

Ingredients:
- 4 tsp. of canola oil
- 2 ¼ lbs. of boneless pork shoulder (Boston butt), trimmed and cut into 1-inch pieces
- 2 cups of diced onion
- 1 ½ cups of water
- ¼ cup of tomato paste
- 2 tbsp. of Spanish smoked paprika
- 1 tbsp. of ground cumin
- 2 tsp. of dried oregano, crumbled
- 1 ½ tsp. of garlic powder
- 3 (14.5-oz.) cans fat-free, lower-sodium chicken broth
- 3 (15.5-oz.) cans white hominy, rinsed and drained
- 1 cup of chopped fresh cilantro

Cooking Instructions:
1. Turn on the Instant Pot to Sauté function and add the 2 tsp. of oil. Add half of the pork and sauté for about 6 minutes to brown on both sides.
2. Transfer the pork to a bowl and set aside. Repeat the same process with remaining pork and remaining pork. Press the Cancel function.
3. Return the pork back into the pot and add onion and following 7 ingredients (through broth). Close and lock the lid in place.
4. Select Manual, High Pressure for 40 minutes. When the timer beeps, do a natural pressure release for about 10 minutes. Carefully remove the lid.
5. Press the Sauté function. Bring the pot to a boil and add the hominy. Sauté, stirring occasionally for about 10 minutes or until thickened.
6. Stir in cilantro and give everything a good stir.
7. Serve and enjoy!

Beef Sirloin Tips

Preparation time: 10 minutes
Cook time: 25 minutes
Total time: 35 minutes

Ingredients:
- 16 ounces of beef sirloin tips (We used sirloin from Butcher Box)
- 2 cups of sliced mushrooms
- ½ medium onion, chopped
- ¼ cup of cooking sherry
- 1 cup of beef broth
- 2 tbsp. of tapioca starch (or cornstarch)
- ½ tsp. of garlic powder
- ¼ tsp. of cracked pepper
- ¼ tsp. of sea salt

Cooking Instructions:
1. Add the beef sirloin tips, sliced mushrooms, chopped onions, and sherry into the bottom of your Instant Pot.
2. In a medium bowl, whisk together the broth and tapioca starch. Pour the mixture into the pot. Add the seasonings and give everything a good stir.
3. Close and lock the lid in place and ensure that the valve is in sealing position. Select Manual, High Pressure for 15 minutes.
4. When the timer beeps, do a natural pressure release for about 10 minutes. Carefully remove the lid and give everything a good stir.
5. Serve and enjoy!

Thai Lettuce Pork Wraps

Preparation time: 10 minutes
Cook time: 30 minutes
Total time: 40 minutes
Servings: 4

Ingredients:
- ½ cup of teriyaki sauce
- 2 tbsp. of rice vinegar
- 1 tsp. of crushed red pepper flakes
- 2 cloves garlic, minced
- ½ cup of chicken or vegetable broth
- 1 tablespoon of oil
- 2 red bell peppers, seeded and sliced into strips
- 2 pounds of boneless pork tenderloin, cut into 2 inch chunks
- ½ cup of reduced fat creamy peanut butter
- 1 tablespoon of water
- 1 tablespoon of cornstarch
- 12-15 lettuce wraps
- Sesame seeds

Cooking Instructions:
1. In a medium bowl, add together the teriyaki sauce, rice vinegar, red pepper flakes, broth, and garlic.
2. Give everything a good whisk to combine and reserve aside. Add the oil, pork and red peppers into the bottom of your Instant Pot.
3. Pour the sauce over the top. Close and lock the lid in place and ensure that the valve is in sealing position.
4. Select Manual, High Pressure for 30 minutes. When the timer beeps, do a natural pressure release for about 10 minutes.
5. Carefully remove the lid and transfer the pork to a bowl. Shred the pork with 2 forks. Press the Sauté function.
6. In a medium bowl, add together the cornstarch and water and whisk everything. Pour the mixture into the sauce.
7. Add the peanut butter and give everything a good stir to combine. Bring the mixture to a boil.
8. Return the shredded pork to the pork and stir to combine. Ladle into lettuce cups and sprinkle sesame seeds over the top.
9. Serve and enjoy!

Mexican Shredded Beef

Preparation time: 10 minutes
Cook time: 35 minutes
Total time: 45 minutes
Servings: 8

Ingredients:
- 3-4 pounds of chuck roast cut into 2 inch pieces
- 1 tablespoon of chili powder
- 1 ½ teaspoon of sea salt
- 1 tablespoon of olive oil
- 1 cup onion, diced
- 2 tablespoons of tomato paste
- 6 garlic cloves, diced
- 1 teaspoon of cumin
- 1 teaspoon of Mexican oregano
- ½ cup of picante sauce salsa
- 1 cup of beef broth
- Cilantro for garnish
- Limes to squeeze over top

Cooking Instructions:
1. In a medium bowl, combine together the cubed meat with chili powder and salt and toss everything to coat the meat.
2. Turn the Instant Pot to Sauté function and add the olive oil. Add the onions and cook until softened. Add in tomato paste, garlic, cumin and Mexican oregano.
3. Give everything a good stir for about 1 minute. Add in seasoned meat. Pour in salsa and beef broth. Close and lock the lid in place.
4. Select the "Meat/Stew" function and adjust to cook for 35 minutes. When the timer beeps, do a natural pressure release for about 15 minutes.
5. Carefully remove the lid and transfer the meat to a bowl. Shred the meat with 2 forks and use leftover liquid as a gravy if desired. Season with salt and pepper.
6. Ladle into serving bowl and top with chopped cilantro and a squeeze of fresh lime juice.
7. Serve immediately and enjoy!

Salsa Pork Chops

Yield: 6
Preparation time: 5 minutes
Cook time: 15 minutes
Total time: 20 minutes

Ingredients:
- 6 bone-in center cut pork chops, about ½ inch thick
- Kosher salt
- Black pepper to taste
- 3 tbsp. of olive oil
- 1 - 24 ounces of jar chunky salsa (We used a zesty cilantro)

Cooking Instructions:
1. Generously season the pork chops with salt and pepper on each side. Press the Sauté function on your Instant Pot and add the olive oil.
2. Add the pork chops in batches once the oil is hot. Sauté each pork chop for about 1-2 minutes on each side, working in batches until all pork chops are browned.
3. Return half of the pork chops back to the pot and top with half the jar of salsa. Add the rest of the pork chops and top with remaining salsa.
4. Close and lock the lid in place and ensure that the valve is in sealing position. Select Manual, High Pressure for 2 minutes.
5. When the timer beeps, do a natural pressure release for about 15 minutes. Carefully remove the lid and check for doneness with a meat thermometer.
6. The pork should read about 145°F. Place the pork chops to a platter and drain the salsa with a slotted spoon.
7. Serve over the top of the pork chops and enjoy!

Easy Beef Stew

Preparation time: 15 minutes
Cook time: 35 minutes
Total time: 45 minutes
Servings: 6

Ingredients:
- 1-2 pounds of beef stew meat, cubed
- 2 cups of gluten-free beef broth or gluten-free beef bone broth
- 1 tbsp. of garlic powder
- 1 tbsp. of onion powder
- 1 tbsp. of dried thyme
- 1 tbsp. of dried sage
- 1 tsp. of salt
- 2 tbsp. of olive oil
- 1 tbsp. of Worcestershire Sauce
- 1 tbsp. of apple cider vinegar
- Mushrooms, carrots, celery, green beans, peeled sweet potatoes and red potatoes, chopped

Cooking Instructions:
1. Press the Sauté button on your Instant Pot and add the olive oil.
2. Add the cubed beef, salt and cook until browned. Add the mushrooms and cook for a couple of minutes.
3. Add the Worcestershire sauce and apple cider vinegar to the beef and mushroom and give everything a good stir.
4. In a medium bowl, add together all of the seasonings and give everything a good stir to combine.
5. Sprinkle the seasoning blend over the beef and mushrooms. Add chopped vegetables into the bottom of your Instant Pot.
6. Add the gluten-free beef broth over the beef and vegetables and give everything a good stir.
7. Close and lock the lid in place and ensure that the valve is in sealing position. Select Manual, High Pressure for 35 minutes.
8. Select the Meat/Stew function and adjust to cook for 35 minutes. When the timer beeps, do a natural pressure release for about 10 minutes, then quick release any remaining pressure.
9. Carefully remove the lid and stir.
10. Serve and enjoy!

Barbacoa Pulled Pork

Preparation time: 10 minutes
Cook time: 30 minutes
Total time: 40 minutes
Serves: 4

Ingredients:
- 1 tbsp. of coconut oil
- 1 brown onion, chopped
- 700 g diced pork (shoulder)
- 5-6 garlic cloves, roughly diced
- 1 large bay leaf or 2 small ones
- 1 tsp. of cumin powder
- 1 tsp. of coriander seed powder
- 1½ tsp. of chipotle chili flakes
- 1 tsp. of onion powder
- 1 tsp. of dried oregano
- 1 tsp. of allspice
- 1 tsp. of sea salt
- Juice of ½ lime
- 1 tbsp. of honey
- 1 cup of chicken stock
- Handful of fresh chopped cilantro, for garnish (optional)

Cooking Instructions:
1. Press the Sauté function on your Instant Pot and add the coconut oil.
2. When hot, add the onion and sauté for about 2 minutes, stirring occasionally. Add the pork and sauté for additional 2 minutes.
3. Add the garlic and spices. Give everything a good stir and add the remaining ingredients. Press the Sauté button.
4. Close and lock the lid in place and ensure that the valve is in sealing position. Select Manual, High Pressure for 20 minutes.
5. When the timer beeps, do a natural pressure release for about 10 minutes, then quick release any remaining pressure.
6. Carefully remove the lid and using a potato masher to press down the meat and flake it into shreds.
7. Press the Sauté function and sauté the shredded meat in its broth for about 7 to 8 minutes, stirring occasionally.
8. Serve with extra lime wedges and fresh cilantro.

Beef Curry

Preparation time: 10 minutes
Cook time: 20 minutes
Total time: 30 minutes
Serves: 4

Ingredients:
- 2 tomatoes, cut into quarters
- 1 medium onion, cut into quarters
- 4 garlic cloves, peeled and chopped
- ½ cup of fresh cilantro
- 1 tsp. of ground cumin
- ½ tsp. of ground coriander
- 1 tsp. of Garam Masala
- ½ tsp. of ground cayenne pepper
- 1 tsp. of salt, or more to taste
- 1 lb. of beef chuck roast, cut into 1-inch cubes

Cooking Instructions:
1. Combine together, the tomatoes, onion, garlic, and cilantro in a blender jar.
2. Blend everything until all the vegetables have turned to a smooth puree. Add the cumin, coriander, garam masala, cayenne, and salt.
3. Blend the vegetables for additional seconds. Add the beef into the bottom of your Instant Pot and pour the vegetable puree on top.
4. Close and lock the lid in place and ensure that the valve is in sealing position. Select Manual, High Pressure for 20 minutes.
5. When the timer beeps, do a natural pressure release for about 10 minutes. Carefully open the lid and stir the curry.
6. Season with salt and pepper to taste.
7. Serve with naan and enjoy!

Tender Greek Pork

Yield: 8-10
Preparation time: 10 minutes
Cook time: 55 minutes
Total time: 1 hour 30 minutes

Ingredients:
- 3-4 lbs. of pork roast, cut into 2-3-inch chunks
- ¼ cup of chicken broth
- ¼ cup of fresh lemon juice
- 2 tsp. of dried oregano
- 1 tsp. of onion powder
- 1 tsp. of garlic powder (or 2-3 cloves garlic, finely minced)
- 1 tsp. of kosher salt
- ½ tsp. of black pepper
- Flatbread or pitas, tzatziki sauce, lettuce, tomatoes, rice, fresh lemon wedges, optional for serving

Cooking Instructions:
1. Add the pork into the bottom of your Instant Pot.
2. In a medium bowl, whisk together the rest of the ingredients. Pour the mixture over the pork, stirring occasionally to coat.
3. Close and lock the lid in place and ensure that the valve is in sealing position. Select Manual, High Pressure for 50 minutes.
4. When the timer beeps, do a natural pressure release for about 10 minutes, then quick release any remaining pressure.
5. Carefully remove the lid and transfer the pork to a bowl. Shred the pork with 2 forks. Add the shredded pork back into the pot and give everything a good stir.
6. Serve and enjoy!

Beef Stroganoff

Preparation time: 10 minutes
Cook time: 15 minutes
Total time: 25 minutes
Servings: 5

Ingredients:
- 1 pound of beef stew meat, can use ground beef, cut into chunks
- 1 can cream of mushroom soup
- 1 onion, diced
- 1 kg of mushrooms
- 1 tablespoon of minced garlic
- 3 tablespoons of olive oil
- ¼ cup of beef broth
- 1/3 cup of sour cream
- 1 ½ tablespoon of cornstarch
- 1 bag egg noodles
- ½ teaspoon of salt
- ½ teaspoon of garlic salt

Cooking Instructions:
1. Turn the Sauté function on your Instant Pot and add the olive oil and garlic.
2. When the oil is hot, add the beef stew meat and onions. Cook, stirring until meat is browned on both sides.
3. Add the mushrooms cut into halves, cut carrots, and even celery if desired. Add the can of cream of mushroom soup, salt.
4. Add the beef broth and give everything a good stir. Close and lock the lid in place and ensure that the valve is in sealing position.
5. Select Manual, High Pressure for 15 minutes. Meanwhile, boil the egg noodles on the stove.
6. When the timer beeps, do a quick pressure release and carefully remove the lid.
7. Press the Sauté function. In a medium bowl, whisk together the cornstarch and add some hot liquid from the pot.
8. Pour the mixture back into your pot. Add the sour cream and give everything a good stir. Simmer the content to bubble and thicken for a couple of minutes.
9. Season with salt and pepper. Serve over cooked egg noodles and enjoy!

Teriyaki Pork Loin

Preparation time: 10 minutes
Cook time: 8 minutes
Total time: 18 minutes
Serves: 4

Ingredients:
- 1.5 lb. of pork tenderloin
- 1 tbsp. of coconut oil
- ½ cup of coconut amino
- 2/3 cup of pineapple juice
- 1 tbsp. of sesame oil
- 1 ½ tsp. of apple cider vinegar
- 1 tsp. of ground ginger powder
- 1 tbsp. of arrowroot powder + 1 tbsp. of water

Cooking Instructions:
1. Press the Sauté function on your Instant Pot and add the 1 tbsp. of coconut oil.
2. When the oil is hot, add the pork tenderloin and sauté for about 2 minutes on each side.
3. Add the coconut amino, pineapple juice, sesame oil, apple cider vinegar, and ground ginger powder.
4. Close and lock the lid in place and ensure that the valve is in sealing position. Select Manual, High Pressure for 8 minutes.
5. When the timer beeps, do a quick pressure release. Carefully remove the lid and transfer the pork to a bowl.
6. Use a meat thermometer to measure and ensure that the internal temperature is at least 145 degrees.
7. In a medium bowl, combine together 1 tbsp. of arrowroot powder and 1 tbsp. of water. Pour the mixture into the pot and whisk until thickened.
8. Serve over cauliflower rice or steamed vegetables and add the sauce to top. Serve immediately and enjoy!

Beef Short Ribs

Servings: 3 - 4
Preparation time: 10 minutes
Cook time: 40 minutes
Total time: 50 minutes

Ingredients:
- 1 tsp. of rosemary
- 1 tsp. of onion salt
- ½ tsp. of paprika
- ½ tsp. of ground pepper
- ½ tsp. of sage
- 2 pounds of beef short rib
- 2 tbsp. of high temperature oil
- 1 6 ounces can tomato paste
- ½ cup of water
- ½ cup of balsamic vinegar
- 2 tbsp. of Dijon mustard
- 1 tbsp. of unsweetened cocoa powder
- 6 cloves garlic

Cooking Instructions:
1. In a medium bowl, mix together the first five ingredients and season beef short rib; set aside.
2. Turn the Instant Pot to Sauté function and add the oil. Place the short ribs with tongs into the Instant Pot. Sauté the short ribs on each side. Remove and set aside.
3. Add the tomato paste, water, balsamic, Dijon mustard, cocoa, and garlic into the bottom of your Instant Pot. Give everything a good mix to combine.
4. Return the short ribs into the pot. Close and lock the lid in place and ensure that the valve is in sealing position.
5. Select Manual, High Pressure for 40 minutes. When the timer beeps, do a natural pressure release for about 10 minutes, then quick release any remaining pressure.
6. Carefully remove the lid and ladle the sauce over each piece of beef short rib.
7. Serve warm and enjoy!

Pork Loin, Stuffing & Gravy

Preparation time: 10 minutes
Cook time: 1 hour 15 minutes
Total time: 1 hour 25 minutes
Servings: 6

Ingredients:
- 4 tablespoons of butter, divided
- 24 ounces of pre-seasoned pork loin, not tenderloin
- 1 small onion, diced
- 6 ounces box of stuffing mix
- 2 ¼ cup of chicken broth
- 2 tablespoons of flour

Cooking Instructions:
1. Press the Sauté function on your Instant Pot and add the 2 tablespoons of butter. When the butter is hot, add the pork loin and cook for about 4 minutes.
2. Cook, stirring and add the onions. Sauté for additional 4 minutes. Add the chicken broth. Close and lock the lid in place and ensure that the valve is in sealing position.
3. Select Manual, High Pressure for 35 minutes. When the timer beeps, do a natural pressure release for about 15 minutes.
4. Transfer the pork loin and set on a cutting board to cool. Shred the pork loin with 2 forks. Scoop 2 cups of hot liquid from the pot and set aside for gravy.
5. Add the box of the stuffing mix to the rest of the liquid in the pot and onions. Give everything a good stir to moisten.
6. Close and lock the lid in place and allow to rest for about 5 minutes. Fluff the stuffing and add to a bowl.
7. Add the rest of 2 tablespoons of butter into the bottom of your Instant Pot. Press the Sauté function. Cook to melt the butter and add the flour.
8. Give everything a good whisk for about 1 minute. Add the reserved 2 cups of broth, and give everything a good stir to combine.
9. Sauté for about 1-2 minutes until thickened. Season with salt and pepper to taste. Return the pork loin back into the pot and stir.
10. Serve with the gravy and stuffing.

Corned Beef and Cabbage

Preparation time: 5 minutes
Cook time: 1 hour 35 minutes
Total time: 1 hour 40 minutes
Servings: 6
Ingredients:
- 2-3 pounds of corned beef, rinsed
- ½ head cabbage, cut in half
- 1 onion, quartered
- 2 potatoes large baking potatoes, cut into half
- 12 ounces of beer or water or beef broth

Cooking Instructions:
1. First, cut the potatoes in half and add them into the bottom of your Instant Pot with the cut side down.
2. Place the corned beef on top of the potatoes. Add the flat beer, beef broth or water on top. Sprinkle the corned beef seasoning packet on top of meat in the pot.
3. Close and lock the lid in place and ensure that the valve is in sealing position. Select Manual, High Pressure for 90 minutes.
4. When the timer beeps, do a natural pressure release for about 15 minutes. Carefully remove the lid and transfer the corned beef to a bowl and set aside.
5. Add the quartered onion into pot with liquid. Add the cut cabbage and separate leaves. Place them on top of potatoes and onions.
6. Close and lock the lid in place and ensure that the valve is in sealing position. Select Manual, High Pressure for 5 minutes.
7. When the timer beeps, do a quick pressure release. Carefully remove the lid and transfer the meat to a cutting board.
8. Shred the meat with 2 forks. Return the meat back into the pot and give everything a good stir.
9. Serve with vegetables on the side and enjoy!

Japanese Pork Tender Rib Stew

Preparation time: 10 minutes
Cook time: 60 minutes
Total time: 70 minutes
Servings: 2 - 3

Ingredients:
- 820 gm of soft pork ribs (pork cartilage)
- 4 slices ginger
- 1 clove garlic, minced
- 3 tablespoons of Japanese salt-reduced light soy sauce
- 2 tablespoons of mirin
- 1 tablespoon of cooking rice wine
- 3 teaspoons of white vinegar
- ½ tablespoon of rock sugar, pounded
- 1 cup of water
- 400 gm radish, peeled and chopped
- Salt, to taste
- Spring onion, for garnish
- 2 teaspoons of corn flour / corn starch
- 1 tablespoon of water

Cooking Instructions:
1. Rinse the pork ribs and drain. Reserve the pork ribs aside. Turn the Instant Pot to Sauté function and add the oil.
2. Sauté the pork ribs on each side, working in batches. Place all the pork ribs into the bottom of your Instant Pot.
3. Add in ginger, garlic, soy sauce, mirin, wine, vinegar, rock sugar and water. Close and lock the lid in place and ensure that that the valve is in sealing position.
4. Select the "Meat/Stew" function and adjust to cook for 35 minutes. When the timer beeps, do a quick pressure release.
5. Carefully remove the lid and add in the radish. Close and lock the lid in place and ensure that the valve is in sealing position.
6. Select the "Meat/Stew" function and adjust to cook for 10 minutes. When the timer beeps, do a quick pressure release.
7. Carefully remove the lid. Turn the Instant Pot to Sauté function. In a medium bowl, mix together the 2 teaspoons of corn flour or corn starch and 1 tablespoon of water.
8. Pour the mixture into the pot and give everything a good stir to thicken. Season with salt and pepper to taste. Garnish with spring onion.
9. Serve warm and enjoy!

Beef Masala Curry

Preparation time: 10 minutes
Cook time: 30 minutes
Total time: 40 minutes

Ingredients:
- 2 pounds of stewing beef, cut in 2 inch cubes
- 1 medium onion, chopped
- 3 garlic cloves, minced
- ½ cup of crushed tomatoes
- ¼ cup of fresh cilantro, chopped
- 1 teaspoon of salt
- 1 teaspoon of freshly ground black pepper
- 1 teaspoon of turmeric
- 1 tablespoon of garam masala
- ½ teaspoon of cumin
- ½ teaspoon of coriander
- ½ teaspoon of cayenne pepper
- ½ teaspoon of smoked paprika
- ½ teaspoon of lemon zest
- 1 teaspoon of brown sugar
- 1 tablespoon of oil
- 1 cup of beef stock

Cooking Instructions:
1. Press the Sauté function on your Instant Pot and add the oil.
2. When the oil is hot, add the chopped onions, garlic, spices, salt and pepper. Sauté for about 3 minutes or until the onions have turned translucent.
3. Add the crushed tomatoes, brown sugar and bring the pot to a boil. Pour the mixture into your food processor and blend everything into a paste.
4. Sauté the meat to brown on both sides. Pour in the blended spice paste, stock and add lemon zest.
5. Close and lock the lid in place and ensure that the valve is in sealing position. Select Manual, High Pressure for 30 minutes. Carefully remove the lid.
6. Serve with steamed rice and chopped cilantro.

INSTANT POT EGG RECIPES

Bacon and Egg Risotto

Preparation time: 10 minutes
Cook time: 5 minutes
Total time: 15 minutes
Servings: 2

Ingredients:
- 3 slices of center cut bacon, chopped
- 1/3 cup of chopped onion
- ¾ cup of Arborio Rice
- 3 tbsp. of Dry White Wine
- 1 ½ cups of chicken broth
- 2 eggs
- 2 tbsp. of grated parmesan cheese
- Salt to taste
- Pepper, to taste
- Chives, for garnish

Cooking Instructions:
1. Press the "Sauté" function on your Instant Pot and add the bacon. Sauté for about 5 minutes or until fat begins to render and bacon is crisping.
2. Add the onion and sauté for additional 2 minutes. Add the rice and cook for 1 minute.
3. Pour in the wine and deglaze the pot to remove any browned bit stuck to the bottom of the pot.
4. Pour in the chicken broth when the wine has been absorbed and give everything a good stir.
5. Close and lock the lid in place and ensure that the valve is in sealing position.
6. Select Manual, High Pressure for 5 minutes. Meanwhile, cook the eggs to your desired choice like poached, sunny side up, over easy etc.
7. When the timer beeps, do a natural pressure release for about 10 minutes. Carefully open the lid and add the parmesan cheese.
8. Season with salt and pepper. Divide between two bowls, add the cooked egg, and sprinkle with chives.
9. Serve and enjoy!

Hard Boiled Eggs

Preparation time: 10 minutes
Cook time: 5 minutes
Total time: 15 minutes

Ingredients:
- 12 eggs
- 1 cup of water

Cooking Instructions:
1. Pour 1 cup of water into the bottom of your Instant Pot and place the steam rack.
2. Place the egg in the steam rack. Close and lock the lid in place and ensure that the valve is in sealing position.
3. Select Manual, High Pressure for 5 minutes. When the timer beeps, do a natural pressure release for about 5 minutes, then quick release any remaining pressure.
4. Carefully open the lid and remove eggs from Instant Pot. Place the eggs in a bowl with cold water. Allow to rest for about 5 minutes.
5. Remove eggs from the bowl. Crack egg on counter top and remove shell.
6. Serve and enjoy!

Egg Bake

Preparation time: 5 minutes
Cook time: 20 minutes
Total time: 25 minutes
Servings: 4

Ingredients:
- 6 slices of bacon, chopped into bite pieces
- 2 cups of frozen hash browns
- 6 eggs
- ¼ cup of milk
- ½ cup of shredded cheddar cheese
- 1 tsp. of kosher salt
- ½ tsp. of pepper
- Onion, red pepper, spinach, mushrooms, green onions, optional

Cooking Instructions:
1. Press the Sauté function on your Instant Pot and add the bacon. Cook the bacon until crispy.
2. Add in your desired veggies and cook for about 3 minutes or until tender. Add in frozen hash browns and give everything a good stir until slightly thawed, for about 2 minutes.
3. Grease a heat metal bowl that will fit into the bottom of your Instant Pot. In a medium bowl, whisk together the eggs, milk, shredded cheese, and salt and pepper.
4. Add the bacon and veggie mixture to the eggs. Pour the egg mixture into the greased, metal bowl. Add 1 ½ cups of water into the bottom of your Instant Pot and place the trivet.
5. Place the metal bowl containing the egg mixture on top of trivet. Close and lock the lid in place and ensure that the valve is in sealing position.
6. Select Manual, High Pressure for 20 minutes. When the timer beeps, do a quick pressure release. Loosen edges and flip over onto a serving bowl.
7. Serve with green onions and extra shredded cheese!

Crustless Quiche

Preparation time: 10 minutes
Cook time: 30 minutes
Total time: 40 minutes
Servings: 4

Ingredients:
- 6 large eggs, well beaten
- ½ cup of milk
- ¼ tsp. of salt
- 1/8 tsp. of ground black pepper
- 4 slices bacon, cooked and crumbled
- 1 cup of cooked ground sausage
- ½ cup of diced ham
- 2 large green onions, chopped
- 1 cup of shredded cheese

Cooking Instructions:
1. Place the metal trivet into the bottom of your Instant Pot and pour 1 cup of water.
2. In a medium bowl, whisk together the eggs, milk, salt, and pepper. Add the bacon, sausage, ham, green onions, and cheese to a 1 ½ quart soufflé dish and give everything a good mix.
3. Pour the egg mixture over the top of the meat and give everything a good stir to combine. Loosely cover the soufflé dish with a piece of aluminum foil.
4. Place the soufflé dish on the trivet in the bottom of your Instant Pot. Close and lock the lid in place and ensure that the valve is in sealing position.
5. Select Manual, High Pressure 30 minutes. When the timer beeps, do a natural pressure release for about 10 minutes, then quick release any remaining pressure.
6. Carefully remove the lid and remove the soufflé dish from the pot. Remove the aluminum foil and sprinkle the top of the quiche with additional cheese, if desired.
7. Place under the broiler and broil until melted and lightly browned. Serve immediately and enjoy!

Eggs en Cocotte

Preparation time: 15 minutes
Cook time: 2 minutes
Total time: 17 minutes
Servings: 3

Ingredients:
- Butter, room temperature
- 3 tbsp. of cream
- 3 fresh pasture raised eggs
- 1 tbsp. of chives
- Sea salt
- Freshly ground pepper
- 1 cup of water

Cooking Instructions:
1. Wipe the sides and bottoms of the ramekins with butter and use a paper towel.
2. Add 1 tbsp. of cream into each of the ramekin. Crack an egg into each of the ramekin and sprinkle with chives.
3. Place the steam rack into the bottom of your Instant Pot and pour 1 cup of water. Place the ramekins on top of the steam rack.
4. Close and lock the lid in place and ensure that the valve is in sealing position. Select Manual, High Pressure for 2 minutes.
5. When the timer beeps, do a quick pressure release. Carefully open the lid and remove the ramekins with hot pad.
6. Season with sea salt and pepper.
7. Serve on toast if desired and enjoy!

Ham and Egg Casserole

Preparation time: 10 minutes
Cook time: 25 minutes
Total time: 35 minutes

Ingredients:
- 4 medium red potatoes
- ½ medium onion, diced
- 1 cup of chopped ham
- 2 cups of shredded cheddar cheese
- 10 large eggs
- 1 cup of milk (We used skim)
- 1 tsp. of salt
- 1 tsp. of pepper

Cooking Instructions:
1. Spray a heat proof bowl that will into the bottom of your Instant Pot with nonstick cooking spray.
2. Place the eggs and milk into the bowl and give everything a good whisk to blend. Add the potatoes, ham, onions, cheese, and salt and pepper in with the eggs.
3. Give everything a good mix to cover everything with the egg mixture. Cover the heat proof bowl with a piece of aluminum foil.
4. Place the steam rack into the bottom of your Instant Pot and pour 2 cups of water. Place the foil covered bowl on top of the steam rack.
5. Close and lock the lid in place and ensure that the valve is in sealing position. Select Manual, High Pressure for 25 minutes.
6. When the timer beeps, do a quick pressure release. Carefully open the lid and covered heat proof bowl and allow to rest.
7. Serve with your desired topping such as sour cream, salsa, avocado, more cheese tomatoes, and salt and pepper!

Mini Fiittatas

Preparation time: 10 minutes
Cook time: 10 minutes
Total time: 20 minutes
Yield: 3

Ingredients:
- 4 slices turkey bacon chopped, uncooked
- 6 eggs
- 1 tsp. of salt
- 1 tsp. of pepper
- 1 small red potato, diced
- ½ bell pepper, diced
- ½ medium onion, diced
- ¼ cup of milk
- ¼ cup of cheddar cheese

Cooking Instructions:
1. Add the turkey bacon on bottom of three heat-proof bowls or ramekins.
2. Place the diced vegetables on top of the turkey bacon. In a medium bowl, mix together the eggs, milk, salt, and pepper.
3. Pour the egg mixture over the veggies and sprinkle with shredded cheese. Cover each heat-proof ramekin with a piece of aluminum foil.
4. Place the covered ramekin on top of the trivet and pour 1 cup of water into the bottom of your Instant Pot.
5. Select Manual, High Pressure for 10 minutes. When the timer beeps, do a quick pressure release.
6. Carefully open the lid and remove the ramekin. Remove the foil and allow to rest for a couple of minutes to cool.
7. Serve and enjoy!

Perfect Poached Egg

Preparation time: 3 minutes
Cook time: 6-8 minutes
Total time: about 15 minutes
Yield: 1-7

Ingredients:
- 1 – 7 eggs
- Salt to taste
- Pepper to taste

Cooking Instructions:
1. Pour 1 cup of water into the bottom of your Instant Pot and place the trivet. Use a nonstick cooking spray to spray your silicone tray.
2. Crack your desired number of eggs into the holes of the silicon tray and place the tray on top of the trivet.
3. Close and lock the lid in place and ensure that the valve is in sealing position. Select Manual, High Pressure for 6 – 8 minutes.
4. When the timer beeps, do a quick pressure release. Carefully open the lid and check the eggs for doneness.
5. Scrape around the edge of the ramekin with a soft edge knife or spoon and flip over to a serving bowl. Season with salt and pepper.
6. Serve on avocado toast, English muffins, tamales, salads, hash browns, if desired and enjoy!

Cheesy Eggs

Preparation time: 10 minutes
Cook time: 20 minutes
Total time: 30 minutes
Yield: 4

Ingredients:
- 6 slices of bacon, chopped
- 2 cups of frozen hash browns
- 6 eggs
- ¼ cup of milk
- ½ cup of shredded cheddar cheese
- 1 tsp. of salt
- ½ tsp. of pepper
- Onion, red pepper, spinach, mushrooms, green onions, optional

Cooking Instructions:
1. Press the Sauté function on your Instant Pot and add the chopped bacon. Cook the bacon until crispy.
2. Add any of your desired veggies and sauté for about 3 minutes or until tender. Add in frozen hash browns and give everything a good stir until slightly thawed, about 2 minutes.
3. Generously grease a heatproof 1 ½ quart casserole dish that will fit into your Instant Pot. In a medium bowl, whisk together the eggs, milk, shredded cheese, and salt and pepper.
4. Add the bacon and veggie mixture from Instant Pot into the heatproof casserole dish. Add 1 ½ cups of water into the bottom of your Instant Pot and place the trivet.
5. Cover the heat proof bowl with a piece of aluminum foil and place on top of the trivet. Close and lock the lid in place and ensure that the valve is in sealing position.
6. Select Manual, High Pressure for 20 minutes. When the timer beeps, do a quick pressure release. Carefully open the lid and remove the heat proof bowl.
7. Carefully use a knife to loosen around the edges and flip on a serving bowl. Serve with green onions and extra shredded cheese!

French "Baked" Eggs

Preparation time: 5 minutes
Cook time: 8 minutes
Total time: 13 minutes

Ingredients:
- 4 eggs
- 4 slices of meat, fish or vegetables
- 4 slices of cheese, or shot of cream
- 4 garnish of fresh herbs
- Olive oil

Cooking Instructions:
1. Pour 1 cup of water into the bottom of your Instant Pot and place the trivet.
2. Grease your ramekin with a drop of olive oil in each. Place a slice of your desired meat, fish or vegetable.
3. Crack an egg into each of the ramekin. Add sliced cheese, or cream, if desired. Tightly cover the ramekin with tin foil for soft egg yolk and leave uncovered for a hard fully-cooked yolk.
4. Place ramekins in the steamer basket and place into the bottom of your Instant Pot. Close and lock the lid in place and ensure that the valve is in sealing position.
5. Select Low Pressure and adjust to cook for 4 minutes. When the timer beeps, do a quick pressure release. Carefully open the lid and remove the ramekins.
6. Allow to rest for a couple of minutes. Carefully loosen the edges with knife and flip on to a serving bowl.
7. Serve immediately and enjoy!

Mexican Casserole

Preparation time: 10 minutes
Cook time: 20 minutes
Total time: 30 minutes
Yield: 6

Ingredients:
- 8 eggs, well-beaten
- 1 lb. of mild, ground sausage
- ½ medium red onion, chopped
- 1 red bell pepper, chopped
- 1 can of black beans, rinsed
- ½ cup of green onions, chopped
- ½ cup of flour
- 1 cup of Cotija cheese
- 1 cup of mozzarella cheese
- Sour cream, cilantro to garnish (optional)

Cooking Instructions:
1. Press the "Sauté" function on your Instant Pot and add the sausage.
2. Add the onion and sauté for about 6 minutes or until onions are translucent and sausage is browned.
3. In a medium bowl, combine together the flour and eggs and give everything a good mix to combine. Pour the egg mixture into the Instant Pot.
4. Add the chopped vegetables, beans and cheeses, and set some mozzarella cheese aside for garnish. Close and lock the lid in place.
5. Select Manual, High Pressure for 20 minutes. When the timer beeps, do a quick pressure release. Carefully open the lid and remove the casserole from the pot.
6. Flip on to a serving bowl and garnish with the reserved mozzarella cheese, cilantro and sour cream as desired.
7. Cool for a couple of minutes to melt the cheese. Serve immediately and enjoy!

INSTANT POT VEGAN & VEGETARIAN RECIPES

Vegetable Beef Soup

Preparation time: 10 minutes
Cook time: 15 minutes
Total time: 25 minutes
Servings: 6

Ingredients:
- 2 cans petite diced tomatoes
- 32-48 ounces of chicken broth
- 1 russet potato, diced
- 1-2 carrots, sliced
- 2 stalks celery, sliced
- ½ onion, diced
- 1 pound of ground beef or turkey
- 2 cup of green beans, cut into 1" pieces
- Dash of salt
- Dash of oregano
- 1 teaspoon of minced garlic

Cooking Instructions:
1. Press the Sauté function on your Instant Pot and add the beef.
2. Add the garlic, and onions. Sauté until meat is no longer pink. Press the Cancel function. Add all the remaining ingredients on top and give everything a good stir.
3. Close and lock the lid in place and ensure that the valve is in sealing position. Select the Soup function and adjust to cook for 15 minutes.
4. When the timer beeps, do a natural pressure release for about 15 minutes. Carefully open the lid and add a sprinkle of shaved parmesan cheese on top, if desired.
5. Serve and enjoy!

Lentil Coconut Curry

Preparation time: 10 minutes
Cook time: 15 minutes
Total time: 45 minutes
Servings: 4 - 6

Ingredients:
- 1 ½ cups of lentils, green or brown, rinsed and drain
- ½ tbsp. of coconut oil
- 1 medium shallot, chopped
- 3 tbsp. of minced fresh ginger
- 2 tbsp. of minced garlic, about 6 cloves
- 1 tbsp. of curry powder, plus 1 tsp.
- ½ tbsp. of coconut sugar or brown sugar
- 1 tsp. of kosher salt
- ¾ tsp. of ground turmeric
- 1/8 - ¼ tsp. of cayenne pepper
- 1 can light coconut milk, 14 oz.
- 2 tbsp. of freshly squeezed lemon juice, about ½ large lemon
- Cooked brown rice, for serving
- Chopped fresh cilantro, for serving

Cooking Instructions:
1. Press the Sauté function on your Instant Pot and add the coconut oil. When the oil is hot, pour 1 tbsp. of water.
2. Add the shallot, ginger, and garlic. Sauté, stirring occasionally, for about 2 minutes or until fragrant and the shallot is soft.
3. Add the curry powder, coconut sugar, salt, turmeric, and cayenne and give everything a good stir.
4. Add the lentils, coconut milk, and pour 1 cup of water. Give everything a good stir to coat the lentils. Press the Cancel function.
5. Close and lock the lid in place and ensure that the valve is in sealing position. Select Manual, High Pressure for 15 minutes.
6. When the timer beeps, do a natural pressure release for about 10 minutes, then quick release any remaining pressure.
7. Carefully remove the lid and stir in the lemon juice. Adjust the seasoning to suit your desired taste. Add more water if the curry is too thick.
8. Serve warm with rice, sprinkled with cilantro and enjoy!

Vegan Quinoa Burrito Bowls

Preparation time: 5 minutes
Cook time: 20 minutes
Total time: 25 minutes
Servings: 4

Ingredients:
- 1 tsp. of extra-virgin olive oil
- ½ red onion, diced
- 1 bell pepper, diced
- ½ tsp. of salt
- 1 tsp. of ground cumin
- 1 cup of quinoa, rinsed well
- 1 cup of prepared salsa
- 1 cup of water
- 1 ½ cups of cooked black beans, or 1 (15 ounces) can, drained and rinsed
- Avocado , guacamole, fresh cilantro, green onions, salsa, lime wedges, shredded lettuce, optional for topping

Cooking Instructions:
1. Press the Sauté function on your Instant Pot and add the oil. Add the onions and peppers and sauté for about 5 minutes or until they begin to soften.
2. Add the cumin and salt and cook for additional 1 minute. Press the Cancel function. Add in the quinoa, salsa, water, and beans.
3. Close and lock the valve in place and ensure that the valve is in sealing position. Select Manual, High Pressure for 12 minutes.
4. When the timer beeps, do a natural pressure release for about 15 minutes. Carefully open the lid and fluff the quinoa with a fork.
5. Serve warm, with your desired toppings such as avocado, diced onions, salsa, and shredded lettuce.

Bulgogi Mushroom Lettuce Wraps

Preparation time: 20 minutes
Cook time: 45 minutes
Total time: 1 hour 5 minutes
Serves: 4 -6

Ingredients:
- 1 yellow onion, sliced
- 1 tablespoon of minced ginger
- 1 tablespoon of minced garlic
- ¼ cup of soy sauce or GF tamari
- 2 tablespoons of rice wine vinegar
- 2 tablespoons of toasted sesame oil
- ¼ cup of maple syrup or coconut sugar
- 2 tbsp. of hot sauce (chili sauce is okay)
- ¼ cup of water
- 1 pound of Portobello or oyster mushrooms, sliced and halved
- 1 tablespoon of corn starch
- 2 tablespoons of water
- 1 tablespoon of sesame seeds + extra for garnish
- 4 green onions, sliced + extra for garnish
- 1 head butter lettuce, romaine or endive
- Fish-free kimchi
- Lime wedges

Cooking Instructions:
1. Add the onion, ginger, garlic, soy sauce, rice wine vinegar, sesame oil, maple syrup, hot sauce, and water into the bottom of your Instant Pot.
2. Give everything a good mix to combine. Add the mushrooms, toss to coat and let to rest for about 15 minutes.
3. Close and lock the lid in place and ensure that the valve is in sealing position. Select Manual, High Pressure for 20 minutes.
4. When the timer beeps, do a natural pressure release for about 10 minutes, then quick release any remaining pressure.
5. Carefully open the lid. Select the Sauté function. In a medium bowl, mix together the 1 tablespoon of corn starch and 2 tablespoons of water.
6. Pour the slurry mixture into the pot and sauté until onions are translucent and sauce thickens, for about 5 mins.
7. Add the sesame seeds and green onions and give everything a good stir to combine. Ladle a few spoonful's of rice in lettuce leaf of your desired choice in a serving bowl.
8. Add a few spoonful's of mushrooms, and top with kimchi, sesame seeds, and green onion.
9. Serve with a wedge of lime, if desired and enjoy!

Cauliflower Tikka Masala

Preparation time: 10 minutes
Cook time: 2 minutes
Total time: 12 minutes
Servings: 4

Ingredients:
- 1 tablespoon of vegan butter or oil
- 1 small onion, diced
- 3 cloves of garlic, minced
- 1 tablespoon of freshly grated ginger
- 2 teaspoons of dried fenugreek leaves
- 2 teaspoons of garam masala
- 1 teaspoon of turmeric
- ½ teaspoon of ground chili
- ¼ teaspoon of ground cumin
- ½ teaspoon of salt
- 1 28-oz. can crushed tomatoes (or diced)
- 1 tablespoon of maple syrup
- 1 cauliflower head, cut into florets
- ½ cup non-dairy yogurt (or cashew cream)
- Fresh parsley, roasted cashews, optional

Cooking Instructions:
1. Press the Sauté function on your Instant Pot and add the oil.
2. When the oil is hot, add the onion, garlic, and ginger. Sauté, for about 4 minutes, or until the onions begin to soften.
3. Add the dried fenugreek leaves, garam masala, turmeric, chili, cumin, and salt.
4. Cook the contents for additional 2 minutes, stirring constantly to avoid burning. Press the Cancel function.
5. Add the crushed tomatoes, maple syrup, and cauliflower florets. Close and lock the in place and ensure that the valve is in sealing position.
6. Select Manual, High Pressure for 2 minutes. When the timer beeps, do a quick pressure release.
7. Carefully open the lid. Stir in the non-dairy yogurt and give everything a good stir to combine.
8. Serve warm with rice, naan, or tofu, and top with fresh parsley and roasted cashews.

Cilantro Lime Quinoa

Servings: 6
Preparation time: 5 minutes
Cook time: 30 minutes
Total time: 35 minutes

Ingredients:
- 4 ounces green chili
- ½ onion, chopped
- ½ bunch cilantro
- 1 ½ cups of quinoa
- 2 teaspoons of veggie bouillon
- 2 cloves garlic, minced
- 1 ½ cups of water
- Juice of 2 limes
- Salt to taste
- Pepper to taste

Cooking Instructions:
1. Add the green chilies, onion, and cilantro in a blender or food processor and blend until smooth.
2. Pour the blended mixture and the rest of the ingredients except for the lime juice into the bottom of your Instant Pot.
3. Close and lock the lid in place and ensure that the valve is in sealing position. Select Manual, High Pressure for 5 minutes.
4. When the timer beeps, do a natural pressure release for about 15 minutes. Carefully open the lid and fluff quinoa and mix in lime juice.
5. Serve and enjoy!

Vegan Alfredo Sauce

Preparation time: 10 minutes
Cook time: 3 minutes
Total time: 13 minutes
Servings: 6

Ingredients:
- 2 tbsp. of olive oil
- 8 cloves garlic, minced
- 6 cups of cauliflower florets (fresh or frozen)
- ¾ cup of raw cashews
- 3 cups of vegetable broth
- 1/2-1 tsp. of salt, to taste
- 1 lb. of cooked fettuccine pasta (whole grain or gluten free if desired)
- Steamed broccoli, kale or green peas, optional

Cooking Instructions:
1. Press the Sauté function on your Instant Pot and add the olive oil. Add the minced garlic and sauté for about 2 minutes or until fragrant.
2. Press the Cancel function. Add the cauliflower, cashews and vegetable broth. Close and lock the lid in place and ensure that the valve is in sealing position.
3. Select Manual, High Pressure for 3 minutes. When the timer beeps, do a quick pressure release. Carefully open the lid and transfer to a blender.
4. Add salt and blend everything in your blender until very smooth. Pour the blended mixture over pasta and give everything a good stir.
5. Add a few tablespoons of water if the sauce is too thick, until your desired level of consistency is achieved.
6. Serve with steamed broccoli, kale or peas if desired.

Vegetable Bolognese

Preparation time: 20 minutes
Cook time: 7 minutes
Total time: 27 minutes
Servings: 8

Ingredients:
- ½ head of cauliflower, cut into rough florets
- 10 oz. of container mushrooms
- 2 cups of shredded carrot
- 2 cups of eggplant chunks
- 46 oz. of crushed tomatoes, 2 – 28 ounces
- 1 cup of water
- 6 cloves garlic, minced
- 2 tablespoons of tomato paste
- 2 tablespoons of agave nectar or, your desired sweetener
- 2 tablespoons of balsamic vinegar
- 1 ½ tbsp. of dried oregano
- 1 tablespoon of dried basil
- 1 ½ tsp. of dried rosemary
- Salt to taste
- Pepper to taste

Cooking Instructions:
1. In your food processor, add the cauliflower florets and pulse until the pieces are tiny. Add the cauliflower pieces into the bottom of your Instant Pot liner.
2. Add the mushrooms to the food processor and pulse until small. Add the small mushrooms into the pot.
3. Repeat the same procedure with the carrots and eggplant, until all the veggies are minced and add them into the pot.
4. Add in the crushed tomatoes, water, garlic, tomato paste, agave nectar, balsamic vinegar, oregano, basil and rosemary.
5. Close and lock the lid in place and ensure that the valve is in sealing position. Select Manual, High Pressure for 7 minutes.
6. When the timer beeps, do a natural pressure release for about 10 minutes. Carefully open the lid and season with salt and pepper to taste.
7. Add additional oregano, basil or rosemary.
8. Serve and enjoy!

Mashed Potatoes with Fried Onions and Bacon

Preparation time: 5 minutes
Cook time: 8 minutes
Total time: 13 minutes

Ingredients:
- 2 ½ lb. of Yukon potatoes, small
- Enough water to cover
- 2 tbsp. of olive oil
- 4 garlic cloves
- 1 cup of plant milk, We like soy
- 1 ½ tsp. of salt
- ¼ cup of nutritional yeast
- 1 cup of canned fried onions (We like the ones from Trader Joe's)
- ½ package, or more to preference, veggie bacon, diced (about ½ cup - 1 cup)

Cooking Instructions:
1. Prepare the potatoes by wash them. Add the potatoes into the bottom of your Instant Pot.
2. Pour enough water to cover the potatoes. Close and lock the lid in place and ensure that the valve is in sealing position.
3. Select Manual, High Pressure for 8 minutes. When the timer beeps, do a natural pressure release for about 10 minutes, then quick release any remaining pressure.
4. Carefully remove the lid and drain the potatoes. Place the potatoes in a bowl and set aside.
5. Press the Sauté function on your Instant Pot and add the olive oil. Add the bacon and cook. Add the garlic and continue cooking.
6. Add 1 cup of milk, salt, and mooch and give everything a good stir. Add the potatoes and mash. Add the extra milk, fried onions and give everything a good stir to mix.
7. Serve and enjoy!

Berry Jam

Preparation time: 10 minutes
Cook time: 10 minutes
Total time: 20 minutes
Servings: 16

Ingredients:
- 1 pound of strawberries, washed, peeled and cored
- 1 cup of blueberries, washed, peeled and cored
- 1 medium apple cored, peeled, and chopped
- ¼ cup of maple syrup
- ¼ cup of orange juice

Cooking Instructions:
1. Add all the ingredients into the bottom of your Instant Pot.
2. Close and lock the lid in place and ensure that the valve is in sealing position. Select Manual, High Pressure for 1 minute.
3. When the timer beeps, do a natural pressure release for about 10 minutes, then quick release any remaining pressure.
4. Carefully remove the lid and mash the mixture to your desired texture. Press the Sauté function. Sauté, stirring regularly for about 8 minutes to thicken the sauce.
5. Allow to rest for a couple of minutes. Store in the refrigerator at least 6 hours or freeze for later use.
6. Serve and enjoy!

Maple Bourbon Chili

Preparation time: 10 minutes
Cook time: 20 minutes
Total time: 30 minutes
Servings: 4

Ingredients:
- 1 tablespoon of olive oil
- 1 medium yellow onion, thinly sliced
- 2-3 cloves garlic, minced
- 4 cups of sweet potatoes, peeled and cubed into 1/2" pieces
- 2 cups of vegetable broth
- 1 ½ tablespoon of chili powder
- 2 teaspoons of cumin
- ½ teaspoon of paprika
- ¼ teaspoon of cayenne pepper
- 2 (15) oz. cans of kidney beans, drained and rinsed
- 1 (15) oz. can diced tomatoes
- ¼ cup of bourbon
- 2 tablespoons of maple syrup
- Salt to taste
- Pepper, to taste
- A few fresh springs of cilantro
- 2 green onions, diced
- 3 small corn tortillas, toasted and sliced (optional)

Cooking Instructions:
1. Press the Sauté function on your Instant Pot and add the olive oil.
2. When the oil is hot, add the onions and cook for about 5 minutes, stirring occasionally, until onions are translucent.
3. Add the garlic and cook for additional 30 seconds. Add the cubed sweet potatoes, chili powder, cumin, paprika, and cayenne pepper, and give everything a good stir to coat.
4. Add the vegetable broth, beans, tomatoes, maple syrup, and bourbon. Close and lock the lid in place and ensure that the valve is in sealing position.
5. Select Manual, High Pressure for 15 minutes. When the timer beeps, do a quick pressure release. Carefully remove the lid and check the potatoes for doneness.
6. If you desired tortillas, grease a cast iron skillet with oil and pan fry the tortillas on each side for about 2-3 minutes until crispy.
7. Transfer to a bowl and allow to cool before cutting into thin strips.
8. Serve with cilantro, green onions, and toasted tortillas.

INSTANT POT APPETIZER RECIPES

Apple Bread with Salted Caramel Icing

Preparation time: 10 minutes
Cook time: 1 hour 10 minutes
Total time: 1 hour 20 minutes
Servings: 10

Ingredients:
- 3 cups of apples, peeled, cored, and cubed
- 1 cup of sugar
- 2 eggs
- 1 tablespoon of vanilla
- 1 tablespoon of apple pie spice
- 2 cups of flour
- 1 stick butter
- 1 tablespoon of baking powder

Topping Ingredients:
- 1 stick salted butter
- 2 cups of brown sugar
- 1 cup of heavy cream
- 2 cups of powdered sugar

Cooking Instructions:
1. In a medium bowl, mix together the eggs, butter, apple pie spice, and sugar until creamy and smooth. Stir in the apples.
2. In a separate bowl, mix together the flour and baking powder. Add the flour mix into bowl containing wet mixture.
3. Pour into a 7-inch" spring form pan. Pour I cup of water into the bottom of your Instant Pot and place the trivet.
4. Place the pan containing the ingredients on top of the trivet. Close and lock the lid in place and ensure that the valve is in sealing position.
5. Select Manual, High Pressure for 70 minutes. When the timer beeps, do a quick pressure release. Carefully open the lid and remove the pan to rest.
6. Top with Icing and serve immediately.

Cheesy Tuna Helper

Preparation time: 10 minutes
Cook time: 4 minutes
Total time: 4 minutes
Servings: 6

Ingredients:
- 1 can of tuna, drained
- 16 ounces of egg noodles
- 1 cup frozen peas
- 28 ounces can of cream mushroom soup
- 4 ounces of cheddar cheese
- ¼ cup of bread crumbs, optional
- 3 cups of water

Cooking Instructions:
1. Add the pasta into the bottom of your Instant pot and pour enough water to cover.
2. Add the tuna, frozen peas, and soup on top of the pasta. Close and lock the lid in place and ensure that the valve is in sealing position.
3. Select Manual, High Pressure for 4 minutes. When the timer beeps, do a quick pressure release. Carefully remove the lid and stir in cheese.
4. Add in a baking dish and cover with breadcrumbs under the broiler for 2-3 minutes if desired.
5. Serve and enjoy!

Cornbread Taco Pie

Preparation time: 10 minutes
Cook time: 18 minutes
Total time: 28 minutes
Servings: 10

Ingredients:
- 1 lb. of ground beef
- 1 box Cornbread Mix
- 1 packet of taco seasonings
- 1 cup of taco sauce
- 1 cup of cheddar cheese
- 1 cup of lettuce
- 1 cup of cherry tomatoes

Cooking Instructions:
1. First, cook the taco meat according to package instructions. Prepare the cornbread mix according to box.
2. Layer the taco meat in a spring form pan and top with the cornbread mixture. Pour 1 cup of water into the bottom of your Instant Pot and place the trivet.
3. Lower the spring form into the pot with a foil sling. Close and lock the lid in place and ensure that the valve is in sealing position.
4. Select Manual, High Pressure for 18 minutes. When the timer beeps, do a natural pressure release for about 5 minutes, then quick release any remaining pressure.
5. Carefully remove the lid and remove the spring form pan. Flip over your taco pie onto a bowl. Top with taco sauce, cheese, lettuce and tomatoes.
6. Serve and enjoy!

French Onion Pot Roast

Preparation time: 2 minutes
Cook time: 1 hour
Total time: 1 hour 20 minutes
Servings: 10

Ingredients:
- 3 lbs. of top round roast, cut into large chunks
- 2 large onions, sliced
- 1 tablespoons of olive oil
- 3 cloves garlic
- 1 tablespoon of salt
- 1 tablespoon of pepper
- 1 tablespoon of garlic powder
- 1 tablespoon of onion powder
- 1 cup of beef broth
- 1 bay leaf
- 2 tablespoons of cornstarch

Cooking Instructions:
1. Add the olive oil into the bottom of your Instant Pot. Mix the dry seasons and rub all over the meats.
2. Add the onions, 3 cloves of garlic and add the meat on top of your onions. Pour in 1 cup of beef broth.
3. Close and lock the lid in place and ensure that the valve is in sealing position. Select Manual, High Pressure for 60 minutes.
4. When the timer beep, do a natural pressure release for about 20 minutes. Carefully open the lid and transfer the meat to a bowl.
5. Shred the meat with 2 forks. In a medium bowl, mix together 2 tablespoons of cornstarch and 2 tablespoons of broth.
6. Press the Sauté function and bring the pot to a boil. Add in cornstarch slurry and sauté for about 1-2 minutes or until your desired thickness is achieved.
7. Pour juices and onions over the meat.
8. Serve and enjoy!

Chicken Pot Pie Casserole

Preparation time: 2 minutes
Cook time: 5 minutes
Total time: 7 minutes
Servings; 6

Ingredients:
- 1 lb. of cubed chicken
- 16 ounces of bag frozen mixed veggies
- 16 ounces of egg noodles
- 1 cup of heavy cream
- 4 cups of chicken broth
- 1 teaspoon of garlic powder
- 1 teaspoon of onion powder
- 1 teaspoon of salt
- 1 teaspoon of pepper

Cooking Instructions:
1. Press the Sauté function on your Instant Pot and add the olive oil. Add the chicken, and spices.
2. Cook for about 2-3 minutes or until the chicken is no longer pink. Add the egg noodles, broth, and veggies.
3. Close and lock the lid in place and ensure that the valve is in sealing position. Select Manual, High Pressure for 5 minutes.
4. When the timer beeps, do a quick pressure release. Carefully open the lid and stir in heavy cream.
5. Press the Sauté function. Sauté for additional 2-3 minutes or until thickens.
6. Serve and enjoy!

South West burritos

Preparation time: 2 minutes
Cook time: 12 minutes
Total time: 14 minutes
Servings: 6

Ingredients:
- 1 medium onion, chopped
- 1 packet taco seasonings
- 2 cups of White Rice
- 1 lb. of ground beef
- 3 cups of water
- 16 ounces of black beans
- 10 ounces of Rotel tomatoes
- 6 Burrito Shells
- 16 ounces of salsa
- Toppings for Burritos like sour cream, shredded cheese etc.

Cooking Instructions:
1. Turn on the Sauté function on your Instant Pot and add the ground beef.
2. Add the onions, half of taco seasonings and give everything a good stir. Add the rice, and water. Do not stir.
3. Add the salsa, tomatoes, beans, and remaining seasonings. Close and lock the lid in place and ensure that the valve is in sealing position.
4. Press the Rice function and adjust to cook for 12 minutes. When the timer beeps, do a quick pressure release.
5. Carefully open the lid and fill each burrito shell with mixture. Add your desired topping.
6. Serve and enjoy!

Bacon and Ranch Salad

Preparation time: 2 minutes
Cook time: 4 minutes
Total time: 6 minutes
Servings: 6

Ingredients:
- 1 box of small shells
- 1 cup of frozen peas and carrots
- 1 cup of mayo
- 1 packet hidden valley ranch
- 3 cups of water
- 6 slices crumbled bacon or bacon bits

Cooking Instructions:
1. Pour the 3 cups of water into the bottom of your Instant Pot and add the dry pasta.
2. Add the peas and carrots on top. Close and lock the lid in place and ensure that the valve is in sealing position.
3. Select Manual, High Pressure for 4 minutes. When the timer beeps, do a quick pressure release.
4. Carefully open the lid and rinse pasta in cold water to cool. In a medium bowl, mix together the mayo and ranch.
5. Give the pasta a good stir with the mayo and ranch mix. Top with bacon bits or crumbled bacon.
6. Serve and enjoy!

Cheesy Taco Pasta

Preparation time: 3 minutes
Cook time: 4 minutes
Total time: 10 minutes
Servings: 6

Ingredients:
- 1 lb. of ground beef
- 1 packet taco seasoning
- 16 ounces of salsa
- 16 ounces of pasta
- 16 ounces can black beans
- 2 cups of Fritos
- 16 ounces of cheddar cheese
- 3 cups of water
- Sour cream
- 4 ounces of cherry tomatoes

Cooking Instructions:
1. Press the Sauté function on your Instant Pot and add the ground beef.
2. Sauté for about 1-2 minutes or until the meat has crumbled. Add the taco seasoning, salsa and black beans.
3. Add 3 cups of water into the bottom of your Instant Pot and add the uncooked pasta.
4. Close and lock the lid in place and ensure that the valve is in sealing position. Select Manual, High Pressure for 4 minutes.
5. When the timer beeps, do a quick pressure release. Carefully open the lid and stir in cheese. Top with Fritos or Doritos, and sour cream.
6. Serve and enjoy!

Homemade Lasagna Hamburger Helper

Preparation time: 2 minutes
Cook time: 5 minutes
Total time: 7 minutes
Servings: 6

Ingredients:
- 1 box Ruffles Pasta 16 ounces
- 8 ounces of ricotta cheese
- 8 ounces of mozzarella cheese
- ½ lb. of ground beef
- ½ lb. of ground sausage
- 32 ounces of Jar Pasta Sauce
- 32 ounces of water

Cooking Instructions:
1. Press the Sauté function on your Instant Pot and sauté both types of meat until just brown and crumbling.
2. Pour in pasta, sauce, and water into the bottom of your Instant Pot. Close and lock the lid in place and ensure that the valve is in sealing position.
3. Select Manual, High Pressure for 5 minutes. When the timer beeps, do a quick pressure release. Press the Cancel function.
4. Carefully remove the lid and stir in Ricotta cheese and half the mozzarella. Pour into a baking pan and top with the remaining mozzarella.
5. Place under the broiler for 2-3 minutes or until cheese is melted if desired.
6. Serve and enjoy!

Loaded Corn Chowder

Preparation time: 10 minutes
Cook time: 20 minutes
Total time: 30 minutes

Ingredients:
- 2 tablespoons of butter
- 1 tablespoon of olive oil
- 1 medium onion, chopped
- 3 red potatoes, cubed
- 3 stalks celery, chopped
- ½ cup of shredded carrots
- 1 16 ounces bag of frozen corn
- 1 lb. of ham steak, cubed
- ½ cup of sour cream
- 2 cups of milk
- 32 ounces chicken broth low sodium
- 2 tablespoons of cornstarch
- 4 slices of thick bacon
- 2 cups of cheddar cheese
- 1 tablespoon of thyme
- 1 tablespoon of oregano
- 1 bay leaf

Cooking Instructions:
1. Press the Sauté function on your Instant Pot and add the butter and olive oil. Add the onions, celery, and carrots.
2. Cook for about 2-3 minutes until onions are translucent. Add the potatoes, ham, frozen corn, chicken broth and the seasons.
3. Close and lock the lid in place and ensure that the valve is in sealing position. Select Manual, High Pressure for 20 minutes.
4. When the timer beeps, do a quick pressure release. Carefully open the lid and stir in milk. In a medium bowl, mix together the slurry cornstarch and broth.
5. Press the Sauté function. Pour the slurry cornstarch mixture into the pot. Stir in cheese and sour cream when the soup gets bubbly and thick.
6. Ladle into serving bowls and top with bacon pieces.
7. Serve and enjoy!

INSTANT POT DESSERT RECIPES

Chocolate Pudding Cake

Preparation time: 10 minutes
Cook time: 25 minutes
Total time: 35 minutes
Servings: 8

Ingredients:
- 1 box chocolate cake mix 15-16 ounces
- 1 box instant chocolate pudding mix 3.9 ounces
- 2 eggs
- ¼ cup of oil
- 1.5 cup of milk or almond milk for dairy free
- ½ cup of chocolate chips semi sweet are great

Cooking Instructions:
1. Add all of the ingredients except chocolate chips in a mixer on. Fold in chocolate chips. Spray your 7-inch spring form pan with nonstick spray.
2. Ladle half of the chocolate pudding batter inside the greased pan and cover the pan with a piece of aluminum foil.
3. Pour 2 cups of water into the bottom of your Instant pot and place the trivet. Place the spring form pan on top of the trivet.
4. Close and lock the lid in place and ensure that the valve is in sealing position. Select Manual, High Pressure for 25 minutes.
5. When the timer beeps, do a natural pressure release for about 10 minutes. Carefully open the lid and remove the pan from the pot.
6. Allow the pan to rest in a cooling rack and remove the foil. Loosen the edges with a knife and flip the cake on a serving bowl.
7. Serve with ice cream on top and enjoy!

Pineapple Upside Down Cake

Preparation time: 6 minutes
Cook time: 25 minutes
Total time: 21 minutes
Servings: 6

Ingredients:
- 2 cups of yellow cake mix or pineapple cake mix
- 2 eggs
- 6 tablespoons of vegetable oil
- 2/3 cups of pineapple juice or water
- 6 maraschino cherries
- 6-8 pineapple tidbits
- 1.5 cup of water
- Vanilla frosting melted, optional

Cooking Instructions:
1. In a medium bowl, mix together the cake mix, egg, oil, and pineapple juice until smooth.
2. Add the halved or whole cherries and pineapple tidbits in a Bundt pan. Pour cake batter on top. Cover the Bundt pan with a piece of aluminum foil.
3. Pour the 1.5 cup of water into the bottom of your Instant Pot and place the trivet. Place the Bundt pan on top of trivet.
4. Close and lock the lid in place and ensure that the valve is in sealing position. Select Manual, High Pressure for 25 minutes.
5. When the timer beeps, do a natural pressure release for about 10 minutes, then quick release any remaining pressure.
6. Carefully open the lid and remove the Bundt pan from the pot. Remove the foil and allow to rest for a couple of minutes.
7. Flip pan over on a serving bowl. Serve with a bit of melted vanilla frosting and pour over top if desired.

Key Lime Pie

Preparation time: 10 minutes
Cook time: 15 minutes
Total time: 25 minutes
Servings: 6

Ingredients:
For Crust:
- 1 cup of graham crackers or vanilla cookies
- 4 tbsp. of unsalted butter, melted

Key Lime Filling Ingredients:
- 3 egg of yolks large
- 2/3 cup of key lime juice (about 8-9 key limes)
- 1 tablespoon key lime zest (about 2-3 key limes)
- 1 (14 ounces) can sweetened condensed milk
- 2 tbsp. of sugar

Topping Ingredients:
- ½ cup of heavy cream
- ¼ cup of sugar
- 1 tsp. of key lime zest, for garnish optional

Cooking Instructions:
1. Use a nonstick cooking spray to spray a 7-inch spring form pan. Blend the crackers in the food processor.
2. In a medium bowl, mix together the graham cracker crumbs with the melted butter. Place the mixture into the bottom and sides of the spring form pan.
3. Freeze while making the filling. Add the egg yolks and sugar in a separate bowl. Mix the eggs and sugar in a mixer on medium-high speed for about 3 minutes or until the yolks turn pale yellow and thicken.
4. Add the condensed milk, key lime juice and zest. Give everything a good mix to combine. Pour the mixture on top of the prepared crust.
5. Use a piece of aluminum foil to cover the spring form pan. Pour 1 cup of water into the bottom of your Instant Pot and place the trivet.
6. Place the pie on top of the trivet. Close and lock the lid in place and ensure that the valve is in sealing position.
7. Select Manual, High Pressure for 15 minutes. When the timer beeps, do a natural pressure release for about 10 minutes.
8. Carefully open the lid and remove the pie from the pot. Remove the aluminum foil cover and refrigerate for at least 4 hours.
9. Serve topped with whip cream and add the sugar until the cream becomes stiff. Add on top of pie and decorate with zest.
10. Serve and enjoy!

Samoa Cheesecake made with Ricotta

Preparation time: 10 minutes
Cook time: 40 minutes
Total time: 50 minutes
Servings: 8

Ingredients:
- 8 ounces of Ricotta cheese
- 8 ounces of cream cheese
- ¾ cup of white sugar
- 2 eggs
- 4 ounces of sour cream
- 2 tablespoons of cornstarch
- 3 tablespoons of flour
- 1 tablespoon of vanilla extract
- 2 cups of crumbled Oreos
- 2 tablespoons of butter, melted

For the Topping:
- 1 can of sweetened condensed milk
- 1 cup of melted chocolate
- 1 cup of shredded coconut

Cooking Instructions:
1. In a medium bowl, mix together the cream cheese, ricotta cheese, and sugar. Crack in eggs one at a time. Add in flour, cornstarch and fold in sour cream.
2. Mix the Oreo crumbles and melted butter together and add into 7-inch spring form pan. Add the cheesecake mixture into the pan.
3. Pour 1 cup of water into the bottom of your Instant Pot and place the trivet. Place the spring form pan on top of the trivet.
4. Close and lock the lid in place and ensure that the valve is in sealing position. Select Manual, High Pressure for 40 minutes. When the timer beeps, do a quick pressure release.
5. Carefully open the lid and remove the cheesecake from the pot. Refrigerate for at least 2-4 hours.
6. Mix together the coconut and caramel spread on top of cheesecake. Drizzle melted chocolate on top.
7. Serve and enjoy!

Pumpkin Banana Chocolate Chip Bundt Cake

Preparation time: 12 minutes
Cook time: 45 minutes
Total time: 57 minutes
Servings: 12

Ingredients:
- ¾ cup of whole wheat flour
- ¾ cup of unbleached all-purpose flour
- ½ tsp. of salt
- 1 tsp. of baking soda
- ½ tsp. of baking powder
- ¾ tsp. of pumpkin pie spice
- ¾ cup of sugar
- 1 medium banana, mashed
- 2 tbsp. of canola oil
- ½ cup of 2% Greek yogurt
- ½ 15 oz. can of 100% pureed pumpkin, We used homemade puree measured on a food scale., 7.5 ounces
- 1 egg
- ½ tsp. of pure vanilla extract
- 2/3 cup of semi-sweet chocolate chips or chocolate chunks

Cooking Instructions:
1. In a small bowl, combine together the flour, salt, baking soda, baking powder, pumpkin pie spice and reserve aside.
2. In an electric mixer, combine together the sugar, banana, oil, yogurt, pureed pumpkin, egg and vanilla and place in another bowl.
3. With the mixer on low, add the dry ingredients until incorporated. Fold in the chocolate chips.
4. Grease the Bundt pan with nonstick cooking spray and pour the batter into the Bundt pan. Cover the Bundt pan with a piece of aluminum foil.
5. Pour 1.5 cups of water into the bottom of your Instant Pot and place the trivet. Place the Bundt pan on top of the trivet.
6. Close and lock the lid in place and ensure that the valve is in sealing position. Select Manual, High Pressure for 35 minutes.
7. When the timer beeps, do a natural pressure release for about 10 minutes, then quick release any remaining pressure.
8. Carefully open the lid and remove the Bundt pan from the Instant Pot. Allow to rest for a couple of minutes to cool.
9. Serve and enjoy!

Crème Brulee

Preparation time: 5 minutes
Cook time: 6 minutes
Total time: 11 minutes
Servings: 6

Ingredients:
- 8 egg yolks
- 1/3 cup of granulated sugar
- Dash of salt
- 2 cups of heavy cream
- 1 ½ tsp. of vanilla
- 6 tbsp. of superfine sugar

Cooking Instructions:
1. Pour 1½ cups of water into the bottom of your Instant Pot and add the trivet.
2. In a medium bowl, whisk together the eggs yolks, 1/3 cup of granulated sugar and salt. Add the cream and vanilla and give everything a good whisk to blend.
3. Spoon the mixture into a large measuring bowl with pour spout. Pour mixture in to six custard cups and cover the cups with a piece of aluminum foil.
4. Stack the cups in a second layer. Close and lock the lid in place and ensure that the valve is in sealing position. Select Manual, High Pressure for 6 minutes.
5. When the timer beeps, do a natural pressure release for about 10 minutes, then quick release any remaining pressure.
6. Carefully open the lid and remove the cups from the pot. Allow to rest for a couple of minutes to cool. Refrigerate covered with plastic wrap for at least 2 hours.
7. Serve and enjoy!

Chocolate Lava Cake

Preparation time: 5 minutes
Cook time: 25 minutes
Total time: 30 minutes
Servings: 6

Ingredients:
- 1 can pie filling 21 ounces, I used cherry
- ½ box of cake mix, about 2 cups, I used chocolate
- 4 tablespoons of butter, melted
- ½ cup of chocolate chips semi sweet
- 1.5 cup of water

Cooking Instructions:
1. Pour the 1.5 cup of water into the bottom of your Instant Pot and place the trivet.
2. In a heat proof bowl, add the pie filling, sprinkle the cake mix on top, and pour the melted butter on top.
3. Sprinkle the chocolate chips on top. Cover the heat proof bowl with a piece of aluminum foil. Place the covered bowl on top the trivet.
4. Close and lock the lid in place and ensure that the valve is in sealing position. Select Manual, High Pressure for 25 minutes.
5. When the timer beeps, do a natural pressure release for about 5 minutes, then quick release any remaining pressure.
6. Carefully open the lid and remove the bowl form the pot. Allow to rest for a couple of minutes to cool.
7. Serve and enjoy!

Lemon Blueberry Breakfast Cake

Preparation time: 20 minutes
Cook time: 30 minutes
Total time: 60 minutes
Yield: 2

Ingredients:
- 2 cups of unbleached all-purpose flour
- 2 tsp. of baking powder
- ½ tsp. of salt
- 1 lemon, zest
- ½ cup of unsalted butter, room temp
- ¾ cup of sugar
- 1 egg, room temperature
- 1 tsp. of vanilla extract
- ½ cup of buttermilk (or your desired milk with 1 tbsp. of lemon juice)
- 2 cups of fresh or frozen blueberries
- ½ lemon, juice (optional)
- ½ cup of powdered sugar (optional)

Cooking Instructions:
1. Grease and flour a heat proof bowl that will fit into your Instant Pot. In a medium bowl, mix together the flour, baking powder, and salt.
2. Set 2 tbsp. of the mixture aside. Add the zest, sugar, and room temperature butter to mixer and beat until everything to combine.
3. Add the egg, vanilla and give everything a good mix to combine. Working in batches or in 1 cup at a time, add the flour mixture and buttermilk to the sugared butter in the stand mixer.
4. Mix everything to incorporate before adding another cup one at a time. Take out the mixer bowl and add the blueberries with the remaining flour and gently fold into batter.
5. Pour 2/3 cup of water into the bottom of your Instant Pot and place the steamer rack. Ladle half of batter into greased heat proof bowl and place into the Instant Pot.
6. Close and lock the lid in place and ensure that the valve is in sealing position. Select Manual, High Pressure for 30 minutes.
7. When the timer beeps, do a quick pressure release. Carefully open the lid and remove the cake. Allow to rest for a couple of minutes to cool.
8. Mix the juice from ½ a lemon with ½ cup of powdered sugar and pour over cake, if desired.
9. Serve and enjoy!

Cookies & Cream Cheesecake

Preparation time: 10 minutes
Cook time: 40 minutes
Total time: 50 minutes

Ingredients:
- 16 ounces of cream cheese
- ½ cup of sugar
- 2 eggs
- 1 teaspoon of vanilla
- ¼ cup of sour cream
- 1 bag of bite size Caco Chocolate sandwich cookies
- 2 tablespoons of butter, melted

Cooking Instructions:
1. Add half of the bag of cookies in your food processor and crumble. Add the melted butter and place the mixture into the bottom of spring form pan.
2. Add together the cream cheese, eggs, sour cream, and sugar in a mix. Give everything a good mix until combined.
3. Stir in sugar and crumble the rest of the cookies. Fold in mixture and pour into the spring form pan.
4. Pour 1 cup of water into the bottom of your Instant Pot and place the trivet. Place the pan on top of the trivet.
5. Close and lock the lid in place and ensure that the valve is in sealing position. Select Manual, High Pressure for 40 minutes.
6. When the timer beeps, do a natural pressure release for about 10 minutes. Carefully open the lid and remove the pan from the pot.
7. Serve and enjoy!

www.ingramcontent.com/pod-product-compliance
Lightning Source LLC
Chambersburg PA
CBHW081746100526
44592CB00015B/2321